Differentiating Instruction With Menus

Biology

ADVANCED-LEVEL MENUS
GRADES 9–12

Differentiating Instruction With Menus

Biology

Laurie E. Westphal

PRUFROCK PRESS INC.
WACO, TEXAS

Dedication

For Laura Osterman, one of my favorite biology teachers!

Library of Congress Cataloging-in-Publication Data

Westphal, Laurie E., 1967-
 Differentiating instruction with menus. Biology / by Laurie E. Westphal.
   pages cm
 Includes bibliographical references.
 ISBN 978-1-61821-078-4 (paperback)
 1. Biology--Study and teaching. 2. Student-centered learning. I. Title. II. Title: Biology.
 QH315.W485 2013
 570.76--dc23
                        2013017466

Edited by Jennifer Robins

Cover and layout design by Raquel Trevino

ISBN-13: 978-1-61821-078-4

Prufrock Press Inc.
P.O. Box 8813
Waco, TX 76714-8813
Phone: (800) 998-2208
Fax: (800) 240-0333
http://www.prufrock.com

CONTENTS

All About Menus and Choice

CHAPTER 1

Choice

"For so many reasons, it is the simply the right thing to do for this age group."

—Shared by a group of secondary teachers when asked why choice is important for students

Why Is Choice Important?

Ask adults whether they would prefer to choose what to do or be told what to do, and of course, they will say they would prefer to have a choice. Students—especially teenagers—have these same feelings. Although they may not always stand up and demand choices if none are present, they benefit in many ways from having them.

One benefit of choice is its ability to meet the needs of so many different students and their varied learning preferences. The Dunedin College of Education (Keen, 2001) conducted a study on the preferred learning styles of 250 gifted students. Students were asked to rank different learning options. Of the 13 different options described to the students, only one did not receive at least one negative response, and that was choice. Although all students have different learning styles and preferences, choice is the one option that meets all students' needs. Why? Well, it takes the focus from the teacher as the decision maker and allows students to decide what is best for them. What teenager would argue against being able to do something that he or she prefers to do? Students are going to choose what best fits their learning preferences and educational needs.

> *"I really was not sure how my students were going to react to these choices. I didn't want the menu to be viewed as busy work when we already had so much content to cover. I was surprised (and relieved) by how well they responded [to the choices]. Now, they want to have choice in everything, which is always up for negotiation."*
>
> —English II teacher

Another benefit of choice is a greater sense of independence for the students. What a powerful feeling! Students will be designing and creating products based on what *they* envision, rather than what their teacher envisions. When students would enter my classroom, many times they had been trained by previous teachers to produce exactly what the teacher wanted, not what the students thought would be best. Teaching my students that what they envisioned could be correct (and wonderful) was often a struggle. "Is this what you want? and "Is this right?" were popular questions as we started the school year. As we progressed and I continued to redirect their question back to them ("Is that what you would like to show?" and "Does that seem right to you?"), students began to ask for my approval less; they became more independent in their work. They might still need assurance, but the phrasing becomes different: "This is what I have so far. Can I ask for help from Joe?" and "I really don't like this; I am going to pick something else." Allowing students to have choices in the products they create to show their learning helps encourage this type of independence in our students.

Strengthened student focus on the required content is a third benefit. When students have choices in the activities they wish to complete, they are more focused on the learning that leads to their chosen product. I know that getting teenagers excited about our content is sometimes a battle, but if the product (e.g., a play, a comic strip, a book) is seen as exciting or challenging, then the battle is half over. Students become excited when they learn information that can help them develop a product they would like to create. Students pay close attention to instruction and have an immediate application for the knowledge being presented in class. Also, if students are focused, they are less likely to be off task during instruction.

Many a great educator has referred to the idea that the best learning takes place when the students have a desire to learn. Some students still have a desire to learn anything that is new to them, but many others do not want to learn anything unless it is of interest to them. By incorporating different activities from which to choose, students stretch beyond what they already know, and teachers create a void that needs to be filled. This void leads to a desire to learn.

A Point to Ponder: Making Good Choices Is a Skill

"I want my students to be independent, and it can be frustrating that they just can't make decisions for themselves. I hadn't thought I might need to actually teach decision-making skills."

—Secondary study skills teacher

When we think of making good choices as a skill, much like writing an effective paragraph or essay, it becomes easy enough to understand that we need to encourage students to make their own choices. In keeping with this analogy, students could certainly figure out how to write on their own, and perhaps even how to compose sentences and paragraphs, by modeling other examples. Imagine, however, the progress and strength of the writing produced when students are given guidance and even the most basic of instruction on how to accomplish the task. The written piece is still their own, but the quality of the finished piece is much stronger when guidance is given during the process. There is a reason why time is spent in the AP classroom focusing on how to write an appropriate response to a document-based question (DBQ) or a free-response question (FRQ). Students need to practice these skills before the big test in May. The same is true with choices; the quality of choices our high school students can make in the classroom is directly impacted by exposure and practice.

As with writing, students can make choices on their own, but when the teacher provides background knowledge and assistance, the choices become more meaningful and the products richer. All students certainly need guidance (even if our strong-willed high school students think they know it all), as the idea of choice may be new to them. Some students may only have experienced basic instructional choices, like choosing between two journal prompts or perhaps having the option of making either a poster or a PowerPoint presentation about the content being studied. Some may not have experienced even this level of choice. This lack of experience can cause frustration for both teacher and students alike.

Teaching Choices as a Skill

So what is the best way to provide this guidance and develop students' skill of making good choices while still allowing them to develop their individualities? First, identify the appropriate number of choices for your students. Although the goal might be to have students choose between 20 different options, teachers might start by having their students choose from three predetermined choices the first day (if they were using a game show menu, for example, students might choose an activity from the first column). Then, after those products have been created, students can choose between another set of three options a few days later and perhaps another three the following week. By breaking down students' choices, teachers are reinforcing how to approach a more complex and/or varied choice format in the future. All students can work up to making complex choices from longer lists of options as their choice skill level increases.

Second, although high school students feel they know everything at this point in time, they still may need guidance on how to select the option that is right for them. They may not automatically gravitate toward options without an exciting and detailed description of each choice. For the most part, students have been trained to produce what the teacher requests, which means that when given a choice, they may choose what seems to be the easiest and what the teacher most wants (then they can get to what they would prefer to be doing). This means that when the teacher discusses the different menu options, he or she has to be equally as excited about each option. The discussion of the different choices has to be somewhat animated and specific. For example, if the content is all very similar, the focus should be on the product: "If you want to create something you might see on YouTube, this one is for you!" or "If you want to be artistic, check this one as a maybe!" The more exposure students have to the think-aloud processing the teacher provides, the more skillful they become in making their own choices.

How Can Teachers Allow Choice?

"The GT students seem to get more involved in assignments when they have choice. They have so many creative ideas and the menus give them the opportunity to use them."

—Secondary social studies teacher

When people go to a restaurant, the common goal is to find something on the menu to satisfy their hunger. Students come into our classrooms having a hunger as well—a hunger for learning. Choice menus are a way of allowing our students to choose how they would like to satisfy that hunger. At the very least, a menu is a list of choices that students use to select an activity (or activities) they would like to complete to show what they have learned. At best, it is a complex system in which students are given point goals and complete different products to earn points (which are based on the levels of Bloom's revised taxonomy; Anderson & Krathwohl, 2001). The menus should incorporate a free-choice option for those "picky eaters" who would like to place a special order to satisfy their learning hunger.

The next few sections provide examples of the types of menus that will be used in this book. Each menu has its own benefits, limitations or drawbacks, and time considerations. An explanation of the free-choice option and its management will follow the information on each type of menu.

Tic-Tac-Toe Menu

"My students really enjoy the Tic-Tac-Toe menus, and I get them to stretch themselves without them realizing it."

—High school AP World Geography teacher

Description

The Tic-Tac-Toe menu (see Figure 1) is a well-known, commonly used menu that contains a total of eight predetermined choices and, if appropriate, one free choice for students. These choices can range from task statements leading to product creation, to complex and/or higher level processing questions, to leveled problems for solving. Choices can be created at the same level of Bloom's revised taxonomy or be arranged in a way to allow for three different levels or objectives within a unit or topic. If all choices have been created at the same level of Bloom's revised taxonomy, each choice carries the same weight for grading and has similar expectations for completion time and effort.

Title

Directions: Check the boxes you plan to complete. They should form a tic-tac-toe across or down. All products are due by _____.

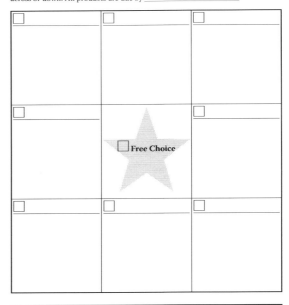

Figure 1. Tic-Tac-Toe menu example.

Benefits

Flexibility. This menu can cover either one topic in depth or three different objectives within one content area. When this menu covers just one objective, all at the same level of Bloom's revised taxonomy (preferably the highest), students have the option of completing three products in a tic-tac-toe pattern or simply picking three from the menu. When it covers three objectives or multiple levels of Bloom's revised taxonomy, students will need to complete a tic-tac-toe pattern (one in each column or row) to be sure they have completed one activity from each objective or level.

Challenge level. When students make choices on this menu to complete a row or column, based on its design, they will usually face one choice that is out of their comfort zone, be it for its level of Bloom's revised taxonomy, its product learning style, or its content. They will complete this "uncomfortable" choice because they want to do the other two options in that row or column.

Friendly design. Students quickly understand how to use this menu. It is nonthreatening because it does not contain points, therefore it seems to encourage students to stretch out of their comfort zones.

Weighting. All products are equally weighted, so recording grades and maintaining paperwork are easily accomplished with this menu.

Short time period. This menu is intended for shorter periods of time, between 1–3 weeks.

Limitations

Few topics. This menu only covers one or three topics.

Student compromise. Although this menu does allow choice, a student will sometimes have to compromise and complete an activity he or she would not have chosen because it completes the required tic-tac-toe. (This is not always bad, though!)

Time Considerations

This menu usually is intended for shorter periods of completion time—at most, it should take 3 weeks with students working outside of class and submitting one product each week. If the menu focuses on one topic in depth and the students have class time to work on their products, it can be completed in one week.

Meal Menu

> *"Seemed pretty easy at first—after all, it was only three things and I was thinking I would just have to draw a few equations. All the lunch and dinner real-world stuff was hard—[I] had to really think."*
>
> —High school Algebra II student

Description

The Meal menu (see Figure 2) is a menu with a total of at least nine predetermined choices as well as two or more enrichment activities for students. The choices are created at the various levels of Bloom's revised taxonomy and incorporate different learning styles, with the levels getting progressively higher and more complex as students progress from breakfast to lunch and then dinner. All products carry the same weight for grading and have similar expectations for completion time and effort. The enrichment options (dessert) can be used for extra credit or replace another meal option at the teacher's discretion.

Benefits

Great starter menu. This menu is very straightforward and easy to understand, so time is saved in presenting the completion expectations.

Flexibility. This menu can cover either one topic in depth or three different objectives, with each meal representing a different objective. With this menu, students have the option of completing three products: one for each meal.

Optional enrichment. Although not required, the dessert category allows students to have the option of going further or deeper into the unit if time permits.

Chunkability. This menu is very easy to break apart into smaller pieces. Whether you have students who need support in making choices or you only want to focus on one aspect of a topic at a time, this menu can accommodate these decisions. Students could be asked to select a breakfast activity while the rest of the menu is put on hold until the product is submitted; once completed, a lunch product is selected, and so on.

Friendly design. Students quickly understand how to use this menu because of its real-world application.

Weighting. All products are equally weighted, so recording grades and maintaining paperwork are easily accomplished with this menu.

Short time period. This menu is intended for shorter periods of time, between 1–3 weeks.

Limitations

Few topics. This menu only covers one or three topics.

Title

Directions: You must choose one activity each for breakfast, lunch, and dinner. Dessert is an activity you can choose to do after you have finished your other meals.

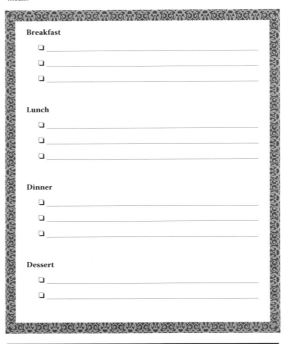

Figure 2. Meal menu example.

Time Considerations

This menu usually is intended for shorter periods of completion time—at most, it should take 3 weeks with students working outside of class and submitting one product each week. If the menu focuses on one topic in depth and the students have class time to work on their products, it can be completed in one week.

List Menu

"I really liked the flexibility of the List menu we used. We actually moved through our unit more quickly than I anticipated so I just changed the points they needed to earn instead of trying to find additional activities for the last two days. It was great."

—World history teacher

Description

A List menu (see Figure 3) has a total of at least 10 predetermined choices, each with its own point value, and at least one free choice for students. There are two versions of the List menu included in this book: the Challenge List menu, which covers one topic in depth, and the Three-Topic List menu, which accommodates three topics. In the one-topic Challenge List menu, topic choices are listed with assigned points based on the levels of Bloom's revised taxonomy. The choices carry different weights and have different expectations for completion time and effort. In the Three-Topic List menu, choices are also assigned points based on Bloom's revised taxonomy and carry different weights; however, the choices are separated by topics listed on the left side of the menu. With both formats, a point criterion is set forth that equals 100%, and students

Title

Guidelines:
1. You may complete as many of the activities listed as you can within the time period.
2. You may choose any combination of activities, but **must** complete at least one activity from each topic area.
3. Your goal is 100 points. You may earn up to _____ points extra credit.
4. You may be as creative as you like within the guidelines listed below.
5. You must share your plan with your teacher by _____.
6. Activities may be turned in at any time during the working time period. They will be graded and recorded on this sheet as you continue to work, so keep it safe!

Topic	Plan to Do	Activity to Complete	Point Value	Date Completed	Points Earned
		Total number of points you are planning to earn.	Total points earned:		

I am planning to complete _____ activities that could earn up to a total of _____ points.

Teacher's initials _____ Student's signature _____

Figure 3. List menu example.

choose how they wish to attain that point goal based on the guidelines set forth on the top of each specific content menu.

Benefits

Responsibility. Students have complete control over their grades. They really like the idea that they can guarantee their grades if they complete their required work and meet the expectations set forth in the rubric. If students lose points on one of the chosen products, then they can complete another to be sure they have met their goal points. This responsibility over their own grades also allows a shift in thinking about grades: Whereas many secondary students think of grades in terms of how the teacher judged their work or what the teacher *gave* them, having control over their grades leads students to understand that they *earn* them.

Different learning levels. This menu also has the flexibility to allow for individualized contracts for different learning levels within the classroom. Even within an Advanced Placement classroom, there can be many ability levels. One way to address this is by preassessing students at the beginning of a unit. Based on the results obtained by this preassessment, students can be contracted (see the bottom of the List menu) for different point goals. If a student shows significant proficiency in the content, then his or her point goal might be 140/140 for a 100%. If the student needs additional practice at a more basic level, then his or her contracted goal may be 75/75 to receive a 100%.

Concept reinforcement. This menu allows for an in-depth study of material; however, with the different levels of Bloom's revised taxonomy being represented, students who are still learning the concepts can choose some of the lower level point value projects to reinforce the basics before jumping into the higher level activities.

Variety. A List menu offers a larger variety of product choices. There is guaranteed to be a product of interest to everyone.

Limitations

Cannot guarantee objectives. If the traditional challenge menu is used for more than one topic, it is possible for a student to not complete an activity for each objective, depending on the choices he or she makes.

Preparation. Teachers need to have all materials ready at the beginning of the unit for students to be able to choose any of the activities on the list, which requires advanced planning. (Note: Once the materials are assembled, the preparation is minimal!)

Time Considerations

This menu is usually intended for shorter amounts of completion time—at the most, 2 weeks.

20-50-80 Menu

"As you suggested, I used one of your 20-50-80 menus as homework to review equations of a line the week before we went into solving systems of equations. It was very easy for the students to understand and saved so much time at the beginning of the systems unit. I am going to use these more often."

—High school Algebra I teacher

Description

A 20-50-80 menu (see Figure 4; also called a 2-5-8 menu, see Magner, 2000), is a variation on a List menu, with a total of at least eight predetermined choices: two choices with a point value of 20, at least four choices with a point value of 50, and at least two choices with a point value of 80. Choices are assigned points based on the levels of Bloom's revised taxonomy. Choices with a point value of 20 represent the *remember* and *understand* levels, choices with a point value of 50 represent the *apply* and *analyze* levels, and choices with a point value of 80 represent the *evaluate* and *create* levels. All levels of choices carry different weights and have different expectations for completion time and effort. Students are expected to earn 100 points for a 100%. Students choose what combination they would like to complete to attain that point goal.

Title

Directions: Choose at least two activities from the menu below. The activities must total 100 points. Place a checkmark next to each box to show which activities you will complete. All activities must be completed by _____.

20 Points
- ❑
- ❑

50 Points
- ❑
- ❑
- ❑
- ❑

80 Points
- ❑
- ❑

Figure 4. 20-50-80 menu example.

Benefits

Responsibility. With this menu, students have complete control over their goals and grades.

Guaranteed activity. This menu's design is set up in such a way that students must complete at least one activity at a higher level of Bloom's revised taxonomy in order to reach their point goal.

Low stress. This menu is one of the shortest menus; if students choose well, they can accomplish their goal by completing only two products. This menu is usually less daunting than some of the longer, more complex menus. It provides students a great introduction to the process of making choices.

Limitations

One topic. Although it can be used for more than one topic, this menu works best with an in-depth study of one topic.

No free choice. By nature, this menu does not allow students to propose their own free choice, because point values need to be assigned based on Bloom's revised taxonomy.

Limited higher level thinking. Students will complete only one activity at a higher level of thinking.

Time Considerations

This menu is usually intended for a shorter amount of completion time—at the most, one week.

Baseball Menu

"Wow! There sure were a lot of choices. I ended up picking the homerun. There weren't very many people who did it because it was pretty long but I really want to go into film production and I wanted to make my own video."

—English III student

Title

Directions: Look through the following choices and decide how you want to make your game add up to 100 points. Singles are worth 10, Doubles are worth 30, Triples are worth 50, and a Home Run is worth 100. Choose any combination you want. Place a check mark next to each choice you are going to complete. Make sure that your points equal 100!

Singles—10 Points Each
- ☐
- ☐
- ☐
- ☐
- ☐
- ☐

Doubles—30 Points Each
- ☐
- ☐
- ☐
- ☐

Triples—50 Points Each
- ☐
- ☐
- ☐
- ☐

Home Run—100 Points Each
- ☐

I Chose:
- _____ Singles (10 points each)
- _____ Doubles (30 points each)
- _____ Triples (50 points each)
- _____ Home Run (100 points)

Figure 5. Baseball menu example.

Description

This menu (see Figure 5) is a base-ball-themed variation of a List menu, with a total of at least 20 predetermined choices: choices are given values as singles, doubles, triples, or home runs based on Bloom's revised taxonomy. Singles represent the *remember* and *understand* levels; doubles, the *apply* and *analyze* levels; triples, the *evaluate* level; and home runs, the *create* level. All levels of choices carry different weights and have different expectations for completion time and effort. Students are expected to earn a certain number of points for a 100%. Students choose what combination they would like to use to attain that number of points.

Benefits

Responsibility. With this menu, students have complete control over their own grades.

Flexibility. This menu allows for many choices at each level. Students should have no trouble finding something that catches their interest.

Theme. This menu has a fun theme that students enjoy and can be used throughout the classroom, especially during baseball season.

Limitations

One topic. This menu is best used for one topic with many objectives for in-depth study.

Preparation. With so many choices available to students, teachers should have all materials ready at the beginning of the unit for students to be able to choose any of the activities on the menu. This sometimes takes some planning because it may require extra space in the classroom.

Time Considerations

This menu is usually intended for a longer amount of completion time, depending on the number of runs required for a 100%—at the most, 4 or 5 weeks.

Game Show Menu

"It was different, doing a [Game Show] menu. I had to really consider how I was going to get enough points but still do all the topics. By the time I was done, at least I knew I got a 100% on a major grade."

—High school U.S. history student

Description

The Game Show menu (see Figure 6) is a complex menu. It covers multiple topics or objectives with three predetermined choices and a free student choice for each objective. Choices are assigned points based on the levels of Bloom's revised taxonomy. All choices carry different weights and have different expectations for completion time and effort. A point criterion is set forth that equals 100%. Students must complete at least one activity from each objective in order to reach their goal.

Benefits

Free choice. This menu allows many choices for students, but if they do not want

			Title			
Topic	Topic	Topic	Topic	Topic		Points for Each Level
☐	☐	☐	☐	☐		15 points
☐	☐	☐	☐	☐		25 points
☐	☐	☐	☐	☐		30 points
Free Choice (prior approval) (25–50 pts.)	Free Choice (prior approval) (25–50 pts.)	Free Choice (prior approval) (25–50 pts.)	Free Choice (prior approval) (25–50 pts.)	Free Choice (prior approval) (25–50 pts.)		25–50 points
Total:	Total:	Total:	Total:	Total:		Total Grade:

Figure 6. Game Show menu example.

to complete the offered activities, they can propose their own activity for each objective.

Responsibility. With this menu, students have complete control over their own grades.

Different learning levels. This menu has the flexibility to allow for individualized contracts for different learning levels within the classroom. Each student can contract for a certain number of points for his or her 100%.

Objectives guaranteed. The teacher is guaranteed that the students complete an activity from each objective covered, even if it is at a lower level.

Limitations

Confirm expectations. The only real limitation for this menu is that students must understand the guidelines for completing the menu.

Time Considerations

This menu is usually intended to be completed for a longer amount of completion time. Although it can be used as a yearlong menu (each column could be a grading period), it is usually intended for 2–3 weeks.

Free Choice

"I try to bring in real-world application for each concept we cover. Sometimes the students simply answer, 'How does this apply to your life?' So, now I let them use the free choice proposals and they can create something to show me the application of the material."

—High school AP Chemistry teacher

Most of the menus included in this book allow students to submit a free-choice product for their teacher's consideration. Figure 7 shows two sample proposal forms that have been used successfully in my classroom. The form used is based on the type of menu being presented. For example, if you are using the Tic-Tac-Toe or Meal menu, there is no need to submit the proposal form for point-based menus. A copy of the appropriate form should be given to each student when the menu is first introduced.

Name: _____   Teacher's Approval: _____

Free-Choice Proposal Form

Proposal Outline

1. What objective, standard, or topic will you be working with?

2. What criteria should be used to grade it (e.g., neatness, content, creativity, artistic value)?

3. What will your product look like?

4. What materials will you need from the teacher to create this product?

Name: _____   Teacher's Approval: _____

Free-Choice Proposal Form for Point-Based Menu

Points requested: _____   Points approved: _____

Proposal Outline

1. What objective, standard, or topic will you be working with?

2. What criteria should be used to grade it (e.g., neatness, content, creativity, artistic value)?

3. What will your product look like?

4. What materials will you need from the teacher to create this product?

Figure 7. Sample proposal forms for free choice.

The form should be discussed with the students so they understand the expectations of a free choice. If students do not want to make a proposal using the proposal form after the teacher has discussed the entire menu and its activities, then they can place the unused form in a designated place in the classroom (I always had a box of blank proposal forms on my supply table so unused forms could be returned there). Others may want to use their forms, and it is often surprising who wants to submit a proposal form after hearing about the opportunity!

Proposal forms must be submitted before students begin working on their free-choice products. The teacher then knows what the students are working on, and the student knows the expectations the teacher has for that product. Once the project has been approved, the form can easily be stapled to the student's menu sheet. The student can refer to the form while developing the free-choice product, and when the grading takes place, the teacher can refer to the agreement for the graded features of the product.

Each part of the proposal form is important and needs to be discussed with students:

- *Name/Teacher's Approval.* The student must submit this form to the teacher for approval. The teacher will carefully review all of the information, discuss any suggestions or alterations with the student, if needed, and then sign the top.
- *Points Requested.* Found only on the point-based menu proposal form, this is where negotiation may need to take place. Students usually will submit their first request for a very high number (even the 100% goal). They tend to equate the amount of time something will take with the number of points it should earn. But please note that the points are always based on the levels of Bloom's revised taxonomy. For example, a PowerPoint presentation with a vocabulary word quiz would get minimal points, although it may have taken a long time to create. If the students have not been exposed to the levels of Bloom's revised taxonomy, this can be difficult to explain. You can always refer to the popular "Bloom's Verbs" to help explain the difference between time-consuming and higher level activities.
- *Points Approved.* Found only on the point-based menu proposal form, this is the final decision recorded by the teacher once the point haggling is finished.
- *Proposal Outline.* This is where the student will tell you everything about the product he or she intends to complete. These

questions should be completed in such a way that you can really picture what the student is planning to complete. This also shows you that the student knows what he or she plans to complete.

o *What objective, standard, or topic will you be working with?* Students need to be specific here. It is not acceptable to write "biology." This is where students look at the objectives of the lesson and choose which objective their product demonstrates.

o *What criteria should be used to grade it (e.g., neatness, content, creativity, artistic value)?* Although there are rubrics for all of the products that the students might create, it is important for the students to explain what criteria are most important to evaluate the product. The student may indicate that the rubric being used for all of the predetermined products is fine; however, he or she may also want to add other criteria here.

o *What will your product look like?* It is important that this response be as detailed as possible. If a student cannot express what it will look like, then he or she has probably not given the free-choice plan enough thought.

o *What materials will you need from the teacher to create this product?* This is an important consideration. Sometimes students do not have the means to purchase items for their project. This can be negotiated as well, but if you ask what students may need, they will often develop even grander ideas for their free choice.

CHAPTER 2

How to Use Menus in the High School Classroom

There are different ways to use instructional menus in the secondary classroom. In order to decide how to implement each menu, the following questions should be considered: How much prior knowledge of the topic being taught do the students have before the unit or lesson begins, how confident are your students in making choices and working independently, and how much intellectually appropriate information is readily available for students to obtain on their own? After considering these questions, there are a variety of ways to use menus in the classroom.

Building Background Knowledge or Accessing Prior Knowledge

"I have students with so many different experiences—sometimes I spend a lot more time than I allotted to review and get everyone up to speed before we get started."

—Secondary social studies teacher

There are many ways to use menus in the classroom. One way that is often overlooked is using menus to review or build background knowledge or access prior knowledge before a unit begins. This is frequently used when students have had exposure to upcoming content in the past, perhaps during the previous year's instruction or through life experiences. Many high school students have had preliminary exposure to the basic information needed in their classes; however, students may not remember the details of the content at the level needed to proceed with the upcoming unit immediately. A shorter menu covering the background or previous year's objectives can be provided in the weeks prior to the new unit so that students have the opportunity to recall and engage with the information in a meaningful way, while not using valuable class time during the first 2–3 days of a unit to do so. Because the teacher knows that the students have covered the content in the past, they should be able to successfully work independently on the menu by engaging their prior knowledge. Students work on products from the selected menu as anchor activities and/or homework throughout the 2 weeks preceding the new unit, with all products being submitted prior to the upcoming unit's initiation. This way, the students have been thinking about the upcoming unit independently for 2 weeks preceding it and are ready to investigate the topic further. By having students use a menu this way, they are ready to take it to a deeper level on the first day of instruction, conserving that much-needed class time.

Enrichment and Supplemental Activities

"Just because my students are teenagers does mean they do not need enrichment—the problem is finding time. My curriculum is so packed and I had always had trouble getting any in. I tried using an enrichment menu for the body systems since I thought we might have enough time. The students really enjoyed it; they seemed to make time for it. I need to use more."

—High school biology teacher

Using menus for enrichment and supplementary activities is the most common way of implementing menus in the classroom. In this case, the students usually do not have a lot of background knowledge, and information about the topic may not be readily available to all students. The teacher will introduce the menu and the activities at the beginning of a unit. The teacher then will progress through the content at the normal rate using his or her curricular materials, periodically allowing class and homework time throughout the unit for students to work on their menu choices to supplement a deeper understanding of the lessons being taught. This method is very effective, as it incorporates an immediate use for the content the teacher is covering. For example, at the beginning of a unit on cellular respiration, the teacher many introduce the menu with the explanation that students may not yet have all of the knowledge to complete all of their choices. During the unit, however, more content will be provided and the students will be prepared to work on new choices. If students want to work ahead, they certainly can find the information on their own, but that is not required. Although some students often see this as a challenge and will begin to investigate concepts mentioned in the menu before the teacher has discussed them, other students begin to develop questions about the concepts and are ready to ask them when the teacher covers the material. This helps build an immense pool of background knowledge and possible content questions before the topic is even discussed in the classroom. As teachers, we constantly fight the battle of trying to get students to read ahead or come to class already prepared for discussion. By introducing a menu at the beginning of a unit and allowing students to complete products as instruction progresses, we encourage the students to naturally investigate the information and come to class prepared without having to make preparation a separate requirement.

Mainstream Instructional/Flipped Classroom Activities

> *"On your suggestion, I tried using the Game Show menu with my geometry unit since I had 3 days of instruction that the students knew well and could work on independently. They really responded to the independence."*
>
> —Secondary math teacher

Another option for using menus in the classroom is to replace certain curricular activities the teacher uses to teach the specified content. If the teacher is using the flipped classroom model, then after students have obtained their basic instruction outside of the classroom, they can be offered choice in their activities during class time. If following a more traditional model, then menus can be used in this way if students may have some limited background knowledge about the content and have information readily available for them among their classroom resources. The teacher selects which aspects of the content must be directly taught to the students and which could be appropriately learned and reinforced through menu activities. The unit is then designed using both formal instructional lessons and specific menu days where the students will use the menu to reinforce the prior knowledge they already have learned, apply the new information, or extend recently presented information in a differentiated way. In order for this option to be effective, the teacher must feel very comfortable with the students' prior knowledge level and their readiness to work independently. Another variation on this method is using menus to manage and incorporate choice into station or rotational activities. Stations have many different functions in the classroom, from reinforcing the instruction that is taking place to allowing students to choose between "resource heavy" (i.e., require a lot of lab materials or equipment) reinforcement activities.

Mini-Lessons

"I have so many different levels in my classroom, using menus with mini-lessons has been a life saver. I actually can work with small groups and everyone else doesn't run wild!"

—Secondary math teacher

The fourth option for menu use is the use of mini-lessons, with the menus driving the accompanying classroom activities. This method is best used when the majority of the students have similar amounts of knowledge about the topic. The teacher can design short 10–15-minute mini-lessons, in which students quickly review basic concepts that already are familiar to them and are then exposed to the new content in a short and concise way. Then students are turned loose to choose an activity on the menu to show that they understand the concept. The Game Show menu usually works very well with this method of instruction, as the topics across the top lend themselves to one mini-lesson per day. Using menus in this way does shorten the amount of time teachers have to use the guided practice aspect of the lesson, so all instruction and examples should be carefully selected. When using the menus in a mini-lesson model, the teacher avoids the one-size-fits-all independent practice portion of the lesson. If there are still a few students struggling, they can be pulled into a small-group situation while the other students work on their choices from the menu.

An important consideration when using menus this way is the independence level of the students. In order for this use of menus to be effective, students will need to be able to work independently for up to 30 minutes after the mini-lesson. Because students are often interested in the product they have chosen, this is not a critical issue, but it is still one worth mentioning as teachers consider how they would like to use various menus in their classrooms.

CHAPTER 3

Product Guidelines

This chapter outlines the different types of products included in the featured menus, as well as the guidelines and expectations for each. It is very important that students know the expectations of a completed product when they choose to work on it. By discussing and demonstrating these expectations *before* students begin, and by having information readily available for students, the teacher can limit frustration on everyone's part.

$1 Contract

Consideration should be given to the cost of creating the products featured on any menu. The resources available to students vary within a classroom, and students should not be graded on the amount of materials they can purchase to make their products look better. These menus are designed to equalize the resources students have available. The materials for most products are available for less than a dollar and can usually be found in a teacher's classroom as part of the classroom supplies. If a product requires materials from the student, there is a $1 contract as part of the product criteria. This is a very important part of the explana-

$1 Contract

I did not spend more than $1.00 on my _____.

_____   _____

Student Signature   Date

My son/daughter, _____, did not spend more than $1.00 on
the product he or she created.

_____   _____

Parent Signature   Date

Figure 8. $1 contract example.

tion of the product. First of all, limiting the amount of money a student (or his or her parents) can spend creates an equal amount of resources for all students. Second, it actually encourages a more creative product. When students are limited by the amount of materials they can readily purchase, they often have to use materials from home in new and unique ways. Figure 8 shows a sample $1 contract that has been used many times in my classroom for various products.

The Products

Table 1 contains a list of the products used in this book, along with ideas for other products that students may choose to develop as free-choice activities. These products were chosen for their flexibility in meeting learning styles and for being products many teachers already encourage in their classrooms. They have been arranged by learning style—visual, kinesthetic, and auditory—and each menu has been designed to include products appropriate for all learning styles. Some of the best products cross over between different categories; however, they have been listed here by how they are presented or implemented in the menus. The specific expectations for all of the products are presented in an easy-to-read card format that can be reproduced for students. This format is convenient for students to have in front of them when they work on their projects.

Table 1
Products

Visual	Kinesthetic	Auditory
Acrostic	Board Game	Children's Book
Advertisement	Bulletin Board Display	Class Game
Book Cover	Card Sort	Commercial/Infomercial
Brochure/Pamphlet	Class Game	Demonstration
Bulletin Board Display	Class Model	Game Show
Cartoon/Comic Strip	Commercial/Infomercial	Interview
Children's Book	Concentration Cards	News Report
Collage	Cross-Cut Model/	Play/Skit
Cross-Cut Model/	Diagram	Presentation of Created
Diagram	Diorama	Product
Crossword Puzzle	Flipbook	PowerPoint–Presentation
Diary/Journal	Folded Quiz Book	Puppet
Dictionary	Game	Song/Rap
Drawing	Mobile	Speech
Essay	Model	Student-Taught Lesson
Folded Quiz Book	Mural	Video
Greeting Card	Museum Exhibit	You Be the Person
Instruction Card	Play/Skit	Presentation
Letter	Product Cube	
Map	Puppet	
Mind Map	Quiz Board	
Newspaper Article	Scrapbook	
Poster	Science Experiment	
PowerPoint–Stand Alone	Student-Taught Lesson	
Questionnaire	Three-Dimensional	
Quiz	Timeline	
Quiz Board	Trading Cards	
Recipe/Recipe Card	Trophy	
Scrapbook	Video	
Story	WebQuest	
Three Facts and a Fib		
Trading Cards		
Venn Diagram		
WebQuest		
Windowpane		
Worksheet		

Product Frustrations

> *"One of the biggest reasons I haven't used more than one product at a time is that I have to constantly reexplain what I want for it. Even if the students write it down, it doesn't mean they won't pester me about it all week."*
>
> —English I teacher

One of the biggest frustrations that accompanies the use of these various products on the menus is the barrage of questions about the products themselves. Students can become so wrapped up in the products and the criteria for creating them that they do not focus on the content being synthesized. This is especially true when menus are first introduced to the class. Students can spend an exorbitant amount of time asking the teacher about the products mentioned on a menu. When this happens, what should have been a 10–15-minute menu introduction turns into 45–50 minutes of discussion about product expectations. In order to facilitate the introduction of the menu products, teachers may want to consider showing students examples of the product(s) from the previous year. Although this can be helpful, it can also lead to additional frustration on the part of both the teacher and the students. Some students may not feel that they can produce a product as nice, as big, as special, or as (you fill in the blank) as the example, or when shown an example, students might interpret that as meaning that the teacher would like something exactly like the one he or she showed to students. To avoid this situation, I would propose that when using examples, the example students are shown be a "blank" one that demonstrates how to create only the shell of the product. If an example of a windowpane is needed, for instance, then students might be shown a blank piece of paper that is divided into six panes. The students can then take the skeleton of the product and make it their own as they create their own version of the windowpane using their information.

Product Guidelines

Most frustrations associated with products can be addressed proactively through the use of standardized, predetermined product guidelines that are shared with students prior to them creating any products. These product guidelines are designed in a specific yet generic way, such that any time throughout the school year that the students select a product, that product's guidelines will apply. A beneficial side effect of using set guidelines for a product is the security it creates. Students are often reticent to try something new, as doing so requires taking a risk. Traditionally, when students select a product, they ask questions about creating it, hope they remember and understood all of the details, and submit the product for grading. It can be quite a surprise when they receive the product back and realize that it was not complete or was not what was expected. As you can imagine, students may not want to take the risk on something new the next time; they often prefer to do what they know and be successful. Through the use of product guidelines, students can begin to feel secure in their choice before they start working on a new product. If they are not feeling secure, they tend to stay within their comfort zone.

The product guidelines for menu products included in this book, as well as some potential free-choice options, are included in an easy-to-read card format (see Figure 9). (The guidelines for some products, such as summaries, are omitted because teachers often have their own criteria for these products.) Once the topic menus have been selected, there are many options available to share the information on the product guidelines.

There really is no one right way to share the product guideline information with your students. It all depends on their abilities and needs. Some teachers choose to duplicate and distribute all of the product guideline pages to students at the beginning of the year so that each student has his or her own copy while working on his or her products. As another option, a few classroom sets can be created by gluing each product guideline card onto a separate index card, hole punching the corner of each card, and placing all of the cards on a metal ring. These ring sets can be placed in a central location or at a supply table where students can borrow and return them as they work on their products. This also allows for the addition of products as they are introduced. Some teachers prefer to introduce the product guidelines as students experience products on their menus. In this case, the product guidelines may be enlarged, laminated, and posted on a bulletin board for easy access and reference during classroom work. The cards for the products mentioned in a specific menu can also be reduced in size and copied onto the back of that menu so they are available when students want to refer to them. No matter which method teachers choose to share the information with the students, they will save themselves a lot of time and frustration by having the product guidelines available for student reference (e.g., "Look at your product guidelines—I think that will answer your question").

Acrostic	Advertisement	Board Game
• Must be at least 8.5" by 11" • Must be neatly written or typed • Target word should be written down the left side of the paper • Each descriptive phrase chosen must begin with one of the letters from the target word • Each descriptive phrase chosen must be related to the target word	• Must be at least 8.5" by 11" • A meaningful slogan should be included • Color picture of item or service should be included • Include price, if appropriate • Can be created on the computer	• At least four thematic game pieces • At least 20 colored/thematic squares • At least 15 question/activity cards • Include a thematic title on the board • Include a complete set of rules for playing the game • At least the size of an open file folder
Book Cover	**Brochure/Pamphlet**	**Bulletin Board Display**
• Front cover—title, author, image • Front inside flap—paragraph summary of the book • Back inside flap—brief biography of author with at least five details • Back cover—editorial comments about the book • Spine—title and author	• Must be at least 8.5" by 11" • Must be in three-fold format; front fold has the title and picture • Must have both pictures and information • Information should be in paragraph form with at least five facts included • Must provide bibliography or sources • Can be created on computer; images from the Internet must have proper credit	• Must fit within assigned space on bulletin board or wall • Must include at least 10 details • Must have a title • Must have at least five different elements (e.g., posters, papers, questions) • Must have at least one interactive element that engages the reader
Card Sort	**Cartoon/Comic Strip**	**Children's Book**
• Must have at least 16 total cards • Should have at least five cards in each column • Can have more than two columns if appropriate • Include an answer key • All cards must be submitted in a carrying bag	• Must be at least 8.5" by 11" • Must have at least six cells • Must have meaningful dialogue that addresses the task • Must include color	• Must have a cover with book's title and student's name as author • Must have at least 10 pages • Each page should have an illustration to accompany the story • Must be neatly written or typed • Can be created on the computer

Figure 9. Product guidelines.

 © Prufrock Press Inc. • *Differentiating Instruction With Menus: Biology • Grades 9–12*

Class Game	Class Model	Collage
• Game should allow all class members to participate • Must have only a few, easy-to-understand rules • Can be a new variation on a current game • Must have multiple questions • Must provide answer key before game is played • Must be approved by teacher before being played	• Must use all class members in the model • Must take no longer than 2 minutes to arrange everyone • Students must be able to understand the part they play in the model • After the model is created, the explanation of the model should take no longer than 2 minutes • Must submit a paragraph that shares how the arrangement of students represents the concept being modeled	• Must be at least 8.5" by 11" • Pictures must be cut neatly from magazines or newspapers (no clip art) • Label items as required in task
Commercial/Infomercial	**Concentration Cards**	**Cross-Cut Model/Diagram**
• Must be 1–3 minutes in length • Script must be turned in before the commercial/infomercial is presented • Can be presented live to an audience or recorded beforehand based on teacher discretion • Should have props or some form of costume(s) • Can include more than one person	• At least 20 index cards (10 matching sets) • Can use both pictures and words • Information should be placed on just one side of each card • Include an answer key that shows the matches • All cards must be submitted in a carrying bag	• Must include a scale to show the relationship between the model/diagram and the actual item • Must include details for each layer • If creating a model, must also meet the guidelines for a model • If creating a diagram, must also meet the guidelines for a poster
Crossword Puzzle	**Demonstration**	**Diary/Journal**
• Must include at least 20 significant words or phrases • Develop appropriate clues • Include puzzle and answer key • Can be created on the computer	• Must be at least 2 minutes in length • Should show all of the important information from the task statement • Must include at least two content-related questions to ask classmates • Must be able to answer questions about the topic being demonstrated	• Must be neatly written or typed • Should include the appropriate number of entries • Should include a date for each entry if appropriate • Should be written in first person

Figure 9. Continued.

Dictionary	Diorama	Drawing
• Must be created in a book format with a cover, a title page, and an about the author page • Should include all of the important words needed to address the task • Definitions are written in your own words • Definitions are easy to understand	• Must be at least 4" by 5" by 8" • Must be self-standing • All interior space must be covered with relevant pictures and information • Name should be written on the back • Informational/title card attached to diorama • $1 contract signed	• Must be at least 8.5" by 11" • Must show what is requested in the task statement • Must include color • Must be neatly drawn by hand • Must have title • Name should be written on the back
Essay	**Flipbook**	**Folded Quiz Book**
• Must be neatly written or typed • Must cover the specific topic in detail • Must be at least three paragraphs • Must provide bibliography or sources, if appropriate	• Must be at least 8.5" by 11" folded in half • All information or opinions should be supported by facts • Must be created with the correct number of flaps cut into the top • Color is optional • Name should be written on the back	• Must be at least 8.5" by 11" folded in half • Must have at least 10 questions • Must be created with the correct number of flaps cut into the top • Questions should be written or typed neatly on upper flaps • Answers should be written or typed neatly inside each flap • Color is optional • Name should be written on the back
Game Show	**Greeting Card**	**Instruction Card**
• Needs an emcee or host • Must have at least two contestants • Must have at least one regular round and one bonus round • Questions should be content specific • Props can be used, but are not mandatory	• Front—colored pictures, words optional • Front inside—personal note related to topic • Back inside—greeting or saying; must meet product criteria • Back outside—logo, publisher, and price for card	• Must be no larger than 5" by 8" • Must be created on heavy paper or index card • Must be neatly written or typed • Uses color drawings • Provides instructions stated in the task

Figure 9. Continued.

Interview	Letter	Map
• Must have at least eight questions about the topic being studied • Person chosen for interview must be an "expert" and qualified to provide answers • Questions and answers must be neatly written or typed	• Must be neatly written or typed • Uses proper letter format • Must be at least three paragraphs in length • Must follow type of letter stated in the menu (e.g., friendly, persuasive, informational)	• Must be at least 8.5" by 11" • Includes accurate information • Includes at least 10 relevant locations • Includes compass rose, legend, scale, and key
Mind Map	**Mobile**	**Model**
• Must be at least 8.5" by 11" • Uses unlined paper • Must have one central idea • Follows the "no more than four" rule: no more than four words coming from any one word • Must be neatly written or developed using a computer	• Includes at least 10 pieces of related information • Includes color and pictures • Includes at least three layers of hanging information • Hangs in a balanced way	• Must be at least 8" by 8" by 12" • Parts of model must be labeled • Should be in scale when appropriate • Must include a title card • Name should be written on the model
Mural	**Museum Exhibit**	**News Report**
• Must be at least 22" x 54" • Must contain at least five pieces of important information • Must have colored pictures • Words are optional, but a title should be included • Name should be written on the back	• Should have title for exhibit • Must include at least five "artifacts" • Each artifact must be labeled with a neatly written card • Exhibit must fit within the size assigned • $1 contract required • No expensive or irreplaceable objects should be used in the display	• Must address the who, what, where, when, why, and how of the topic • Script of report must be turned in with project (or before if performance will be live) • Must be either performed live or recorded beforehand based on teacher discretion

Figure 9. Continued.

Newspaper Article	Play/Skit	Poster
• Must be informational in nature • Must follow standard newspaper format • Must include a picture with caption that supports article • Must be at least three paragraphs in length • Must be neatly written or typed	• Must be 3–5 minutes in length • Script must be turned in before play is presented • May be presented to an audience or recorded for future showing based on teacher discretion • Should have props or some form of costume(s) • Can include more than one person	• Should be the size of a standard poster board • Must include at least five pieces of important information • Must have a title • Must contain both words and pictures • Name should be written on the back • Must provide bibliography or sources, if appropriate
PowerPoint—Presentation	**PowerPoint—Stand Alone**	**Product Cube**
• Must include at least 10 informational slides and one title slide with student's name • Should include no more than two words per page • Slides must have color and no more than one graphic per page • Animations are optional but should not distract from information being presented • Presentation should be timed and flow with the speech being given	• Must include at least 10 informational slides and one title slide with student's name • Should include no more than 10 words per page • Slides must have color and no more than one graphic per page • Animations are optional but should not distract from information being presented • Must provide bibliography or sources, if appropriate	• All six sides of the cube must be filled with information as stated in the task • Must be neatly written or typed • Name must be printed neatly on the bottom of one of the sides • Should be submitted flat for grading
Puppet	**Questionnaire**	**Quiz**
• Puppet should be handmade and must have a moveable mouth • A list of supplies used to make the puppet must be turned in with the puppet • $1 contract signed • If used in a puppet show, must also meet the criteria for a play	• Must be neatly written or typed • Include at least 10 questions with possible answers • Questions must be helpful to gathering information on the topic being studied • If questionnaire is to be used, at least 15 people must provide answers	• Must be at least a half sheet of paper long • Must be neatly written or typed • Must cover the specific topic in detail • Must include at least five questions including a short answer question • Must have at least one graphic • An answer key must be turned in with the quiz

Figure 9. Continued.

Quiz Board	Recipe/Recipe Card	Scrapbook
• Must have at least five questions • Must have at least five answers • Should use a system with lights to facilitate self-checking	• Must be written neatly or typed on a piece of paper or an index card • Must have a list of ingredients with measurement for each • Must have numbered steps that explain how to make the recipe	• Cover of scrapbook must have a meaningful title and student's name • Must have at least five themed pages • Each page should have at least one meaningful picture • All photos and pictures must have captions • Must provide bibliography or sources, if appropriate
Song/Rap	**Speech**	**Story**
• Words must make sense • Must be either performed live or recorded beforehand based on teacher discretion • Written words must be turned in before performance or with taped song • Should be at least 2 minutes in length	• Must be at least 2 minutes in length • Should not be read from written paper • Note cards can be used • Written speech must be turned in before speech is presented • Must be either performed live or recorded beforehand based on teacher discretion • Voice must be clear, loud, and easy to understand	• Must have all of the elements of a well-written story (setting, characters, conflict, rising action, and resolution) • Must be appropriate length to allow for story elements • Must be neatly written or typed
Three-Dimensional Timeline	**Three Facts and a Fib**	**Trading Cards**
• Must be no bigger than standard-size poster board • Must be divided into equal time units • Must contain at least 10 important dates and have at least two sentences explaining why each date is important • Must have a meaningful, creative object securely attached beside each date to represent that date • Must be able to explain how each object represents each date or event	• Must be written, typed, or created using PowerPoint • Must include exactly four statements: three true statements (facts) and one false statement (fib) • False statement should not obvious • Must include a brief paragraph that explains why the fib is false	• Include at least 10 cards • Each card must be at least 3" by 5" • Each card should have a colored picture • Include at least three facts on the subject of the card • Cards must have information on both sides • All cards must be submitted in a carrying bag

Figure 9. Continued.

Trophy	Venn Diagram	Video
• Must be at least 6" tall • Must have a base with the name of the person getting the trophy and the name of the award written neatly or typed on it • Top of trophy must be appropriate and represent the award • Name should be written on the bottom of the award • Must be an originally designed trophy (avoid reusing a trophy from home)	• Must be at least 8.5" by 11" • Shapes should be thematic and neatly drawn • Must have a title for entire diagram and a title for each section • Must have at least six items in each section of the diagram • Name should be written on the back	• Use VHS, DVD, or Flash format • Turn in a written plan or story board with project • Students will need to arrange their own way to record the video or allow teacher at least 3 days notice to set up recording • Covers important information about the project • Name should be written on the video label
WebQuest	**Windowpane**	**Worksheet**
• Must quest through at least five high-quality websites • Websites should be linked in the document • Can be submitted in a Word or PowerPoint document • Includes at least three questions for each website • Must address the topic	• Must be at least 8.5" by 11" unlined paper • Must include at least six squares • Each square must include both a picture and words that must be neatly written or typed • All pictures should be both creative and meaningful • Name should be written on the bottom right-hand corner of the front of the windowpane	• Must be 8.5" by 11" • Must be neatly written or typed • Must cover the specific topic or question in detail • Must be creative in design • Must have at least one graphic • An answer key will be turned in with the worksheet
You Be the Person Presentation		
• Take on the role of the person • Cover at least five important facts about the life or achievements of the person • Must be 2–4 minutes in length • Script must be turned in before information is presented • Should be presented to an audience with the ability to answer questions while in character • Must have props or some form of costume		

Figure 9. Continued.

CHAPTER 4

Rubrics and Grading

> *"One rubric–and I can grade everything? Now we are talking!"*
>
> —Group of secondary teachers

The most common reason teachers feel uncomfortable with menus is the need for equal grading. Teachers often feel that it is easier to grade the same type of product made by all of the students than to grade a large number of different products, none of which looks like any other. The great equalizer for hundreds of different products is a generic rubric that can cover all of the important qualities of an excellent product.

All-Purpose Rubric

Figure 10 is an example of a rubric that has been classroom tested with the menus included in this book. This rubric can be used with any point value activity presented in a menu, as there are five criteria and the columns represent full points, half points, and no points. Although Tic-Tac-Toe and Meal menus are not point based, this rubric can also be used

All-Purpose Rubric

Name: _____

Criteria	Excellent (Full Credit)	Good (Half Credit)	Poor (No Credit)	Self
Content Is the content of the product well chosen?	Content chosen represents the best choice for the product. Information or graphics are well chosen and related to content.	Information or graphics are related to content, but are not the best choice for the product.	Information or graphics present do not appear related to the topic or task.	
Completeness Is everything included in the product?	All information needed is included. Product meets the product guideline criteria and the criteria of the menu task.	Some important information is missing. Product meets the product guideline criteria and the criteria of the menu task.	Most important information is missing. The product does not meet the task or does not meet the product criteria.	
Creativity Is the product original?	Presentation of information is from a new and original perspective. Graphics are original. Product includes elements of fun and interest.	Presentation of information is from a new perspective. Graphics are not original. Product has elements of fun and interest.	There is no evidence of new thoughts or perspectives in the product or any part of the product was plagiarized.	
Correctness Is all of the information included correct?	All information presented is correct and accurate.		Any portion of the information presented in product is incorrect.	
Communication Is the information in the product well communicated?	All information is neat and easy to read. Product is in appropriate format and shows significant effort. Oral presentation was easy to understand and presented with fluency.	Most (80%) of the product is neat and easy to read. Product is in appropriate format and shows significant effort. Oral presentation was easy to understand, with some fluency.	More than 20% product is not neat and easy to read or the product is not in the appropriate format. It does not show significant effort. Oral presentation was not fluent or easy to understand.	
			Total Grade:	

Figure 10. All-purpose rubric.

to grade products from these menus. Teachers can assign 100 points to each of the three products on these menus and then use the all-purpose rubric to grade each product individually.

There are different ways that this rubric can be shared with students. Some teachers prefer to provide it when a menu is presented to students. The rubric can be reproduced on the back of the menu along with its guidelines. The rubric can also be given to students at the same time as the product guideline cards so they always know the expectations as they complete projects throughout the school year. Some teachers prefer to keep a master copy for themselves and post an enlarged copy of the rubric on a bulletin board.

No matter how the rubric is shared with students, the first time they see this rubric, it should be explained in detail, especially the last column, titled "Self." It is very important that students self-evaluate their projects. This column can provide a unique perspective on the project as it is being graded. Note: This rubric was designed to be specific enough that students will understand the criteria the teacher is seeking, but general enough that they can still be as creative as they like in the creation of their product.

Student-Created Experiment and Student-Taught Lesson Rubrics

Although the all-purpose rubric can be used for all activities, there are two occasions that warrant special rubrics: science experiments and student-taught lessons. These are unique situations, with many fine details that must be considered to create a quality product.

By high school, most students have an understanding of the scientific method and are ready to begin their own investigations. Understanding the scientific method, however, does not always guarantee that students know how to apply it to their own investigations. The student-created experiment rubric (see Figure 11) will guide students as they develop their own experiments.

Student-taught lessons are another unique situation. The secondary curriculum is already packed with information that needs to be covered, and turning class time over to students should only be done if it will benefit everyone involved. Student-taught lessons can cause stress for both students and teachers. Teachers would often like to allow students to teach their fellow classmates, but they are not comfortable with

Student-Created Experiment Rubric

Name: _____

Criteria	Excellent	Good	Fair	Poor	Self
Title	**5**	**3**	**1**	**0**	
The title is appropriate; represents lab.	Title is appropriate, unique, and represents lab.	Title is present and appropriate, but not unique.	Title is present, but there is no significance to this lab.	Not present.	
Problem/Purpose	**5**	**3**	**1**	**0**	
Problem stated as question; appropriate for lab. Purpose stated as sentence.	Problem/purpose is present and contains proper punctuation and format.	Problem/purpose is present and contains proper punctuation, but not in proper format.	Problem/purpose is present, but does not contain proper format or punctuation.	Not present.	
Hypothesis	**10**	**5**	**3**	**0**	
Stated as an if/then statement (if appropriate) and relates to the problem.	Hypothesis is present, contains proper punctuation and format, and relates to the problem.	Hypothesis is present, contains proper punctuation, and relates to the problem, but not in proper format.	Hypothesis is present, but no obvious relation to problem. It contains proper punctuation, but not in proper format.	Not present or does not relate to problem.	
Materials	**10**	**5**	**3**	**0**	
All materials present and all exact in description (e.g., "250 ml beaker" rather than "beaker").	All materials present and all exact in description.	Missing no more than one item and all exact descriptions.	Missing no more than one item and 90% of the descriptions are exact.	Missing no more one item but less than 90% of the descriptions are exact, or materials are not present.	
Procedure	**20**	**15**	**8**	**0**	
Procedure is sequential and easy to read. Exact; written in a way that would allow others to repeat the experiment.	The procedure is sequential, easy to read, and contains proper punctuation. The procedure is exact.	The procedure is sequential and easy to read, but missing some proper punctuation. The procedure is exact.	The procedure is not sequential, not easy to read, or missing some proper punctuation, but is exact.	The procedure is not exact, not easy to read, not sequential, or not present.	

Figure 11. Student-created experiment rubric.

Student-Created Experiment Rubric
Continued

Criteria	Excellent	Good	Fair	Poor	Self
Data Table	15	10	5	0	
Data are recorded in an appropriate manner, easy to read and understand, and have proper units, titles, and descriptions.	Data are easy to read, all numbers are entered with units, data table has title, and columns and rows are labeled.	Data table has no title, but is easy to read, all numbers are entered with units, and columns and rows are labeled.	Data table has no title, but is easy to read, no more than three numbers are entered without units, and columns and rows are labeled.	Data table has no title, is not easy to read, some numbers are entered without units, columns and rows are not labeled, or not present.	
Representation of Data	15	10	5	0	
Data are recorded in an appropriate manner, and are easy to read and understand. Graph has proper units, titles, and descriptions, and the proper graph has been chosen.	Data are easy to read; graph has title, units, and descriptors; and variables are on the correct axis. Data are clearly represented.	Data are easy to read; graph has units and descriptors, but no title; and variables are on the correct axis. Data are clearly represented.	Data are easy to read; graph has descriptors, but no units or title; and variables are on the correct axis. Data are clearly represented.	Data are easy to read, graph has missing descriptors, variables are on the incorrect axis, or not present.	
Conclusion	20	12	4	0	
Conclusion is in paragraph form, revisits hypothesis, explains how the lab was conducted, suggests margins for error, and makes a new hypothesis if needed.	Contains proper punctuation and form, describes experiment and points of error, and revisits hypothesis and suggests a new one if necessary.	Contains proper punctuation and form, describes experiment, revisits hypothesis and suggest a new one if necessary, but does not describe points of error.	Missing proper punctuation or form, or revisits hypothesis but does not suggest a new one if necessary.	Does not revisit hypothesis or conclusion is not present.	
				Total Grade:	

Figure 11. Continued.

the grading aspect of the assignment. Rarely do students understand all of the components that go into designing an effective lesson. The student-taught lesson rubric (see Figure 12) helps focus the student on the important aspects of a well-designed lesson and allows teachers to make the evaluation more subjective.

Student-Taught Lesson Rubric   Name: _____

Parts of Lesson	Excellent	Good	Fair	Poor	Self
Prepared and Ready All materials and lesson ready at the start of class period, from warm-up to conclusion of lesson.	10 Everything is ready to present.	6 Lesson is present, but small amount of scrambling.	3 Lesson is present, but major scrambling.	0 No lesson ready or missing major components.	
Understanding Presenter(s) understands the material well. Students understand information presented.	20 All information is correct and in correct format.	12 Presenter understands; 25% of students do not.	4 Presenter understands; 50% of students do not.	0 Presenter is confused.	
Complete Includes all significant information from section or topic.	15 Includes all important information.	10 Includes most important information.	2 Includes less than 50% of the important information.	0 Information is not related.	
Practice Includes some way for students to practice the information presented.	20 Practice present; was well chosen.	10 Practice present; can be applied effectively.	5 Practice present; not related or best choice.	0 No practice or students are confused.	
Interest/Fun Most of the class was involved, interested, and participating.	15 Everyone interested and participating.	10 75% actively participating.	5 Less than 50% actively participating.	0 Everyone off task.	
Creativity Information presented in an imaginative way.	20 Wow, creative! I never would have thought of that!	12 Good ideas!	5 Some good pieces but general instruction.	0 No creativity; all lecture, notes, or worksheet.	

Your Topic/Objective:

Comments:

Don't forget: All copy requests and material requests must be made at least 24 hours in advance.

Figure 12. Student-taught lesson rubric.

The Menus

How to Use the Menu Pages

Each topic in this section has:
- an introduction page for the teacher,
- the content menu,
- specific guidelines for the menu, and
- activities mentioned in the menu.

Introduction Pages

The introduction pages for each topic are meant to provide an overview of each set of menus. They are divided into the following areas:
- *Objectives Covered Through the Menu and Activities.* This area will list all of the objectives that the menu can address. Menus are arranged in such a way that if students complete the guidelines set forth in the instructions, all of these objectives will be covered.
- *Materials Needed by Students for Completion.* For each menu, it is expected that the teacher will provide, or students will have access to, the following materials:

o lined paper,
o glue,
o colored pencils or markers, and
o blank 8.5" × 11" white paper.

The introduction page also includes a list of additional materials that may be needed by students. Because students have the choice of which menu items they would like to complete, it is possible that the teacher will not need all of the additional materials for every student. Some menu options may involve students developing their own experiment. This will also be noted here with materials commonly used by students in their own experiments.

- *Special Notes on the Use of This Menu.* Some menus allow students to choose to present demonstrations, experiments, songs, news reports, or PowerPoint presentations to their classmates. This section will give any special tips on managing products that may require more time, supplies, or space. This section will also share any tips to consider for a specific activity.

- *Time Frame.* Each menu has its own ideal time frame based on its structure, but all work best with at least a one-week time frame. Menus that assess more objectives are better suited to more than 2 weeks. This section will give you an overview about the best time frame for completing the entire menu, as well as options for shorter time periods. If teachers do not have time to devote to completing an entire menu, they can choose the 1–2-day option for any menu topic students are currently studying.

- *Suggested Forms.* This section lists the rubrics and reproducibles that should be available for students as the menus are introduced. If a menu has a free-choice option, the appropriate proposal form will also be listed here.

CHAPTER 5

Biology Basics

Introduction to Biology

Three-Topic List Menu

Objectives Covered Through This Menu and These Activities
- Students will understand the content included in the study of biology.
- Students will investigate the nature of science as it relates to biology.
- Students will identify the seven characteristics of living things.

Materials Needed by Students for Completion
- Poster board or large white paper
- Blank index cards (for trading cards)
- Aluminum foil (for quiz boards)
- Holiday lights (for quiz boards)
- Wires (for quiz boards)
- Microsoft PowerPoint or other slideshow software
- DVD or VHS recorder (for infomercials)
- Scrapbooking materials
- Materials for bulletin board displays

Special Notes on the Use of This Menu
- This menu gives students the opportunity to create an infomercial. Although students enjoy producing their own videos, there often are difficulties obtaining the equipment and scheduling the use of a video recorder. This activity can be modified by allowing students to act out the infomercial (like a play) or, if students have the technology, allowing them to produce a webcam version of their product.
- This menu allows students to create a bulletin board display. Some classrooms may only have one bulletin board, so the teacher can divide the board into sections, or additional classroom wall or hall space can be sectioned off for the creation of these displays. Students can plan their display based on the amount of space they are assigned.
- This menu gives students an opportunity to create a quiz board. A student-friendly information sheet that offers the steps for constructing a quiz board is available at http://www.cesiscience.org/attachments/article/100/QuizBoardDirections.pdf.

Time Frame

- 1–2 weeks—Students are given the menu as the unit is started, and the guidelines and point expectations are discussed. Students will need to earn 100 points for 100%, although there is an opportunity for extra credit if the teacher would like to use another target number. Because this menu covers three topics in depth, the teacher may choose to only go over the options for the topic being covered first; the students place check marks in the boxes next to the activities they are most interested in completing. As instruction continues, additional explanation of the new topic activities can be provided. Once students have access to the entire menu, teachers will need to set aside a few moments to sign the agreement at the bottom of the page with each student. As students complete activities, they will be submitted to the teacher for grading.
- 1–2 days—The teacher chooses an activity or product from an objective to use with the entire class during that lesson time.

Suggested Forms

- All-purpose rubric
- Proposal form for point-based products

Name:_____ Date:_____

Introduction to Biology

Guidelines:

1. You may complete as many of the activities listed as you can within the time period.
2. You may choose any combination of activities, but you **must** complete at least one activity from each topic area.
3. Your goal is 100 points. You may earn up to _____ points extra credit.
4. You may be as creative as you like within the guidelines listed below.
5. You must share your plan with your teacher by _____.
6. Activities may be turned in at any time during the working time period. They will be graded and recorded on this sheet as you continue to work, so keep it safe!

Topic	Plan to Do	Activity to Complete	Point Value	Date Completed	Points Earned
What Is Biology?		Write an acrostic for the word *biology*. Each word or phrase should be related to what biology studies.	10		
		Draw a mind map that shows the different areas of biology and what is studied in each.	10		
		Select a biologist who is currently doing research in an area that interests you. Design a bulletin board display about his or her work.	20		
		Create a PowerPoint presentation that could be used at your school's open house to tell parents about the content being covered in biology classes.	20		
		Write a children's book to teach elementary school students that biology is a science they encounter every day.	25		
Nature of Science		Create three facts and a fib about what people believe science to be.	15		
		Design a quiz board to quiz your classmates on what science is and is not.	20		
		Collect at least 10 quotes in which famous scientists and historians share their opinions of science. Make a set of trading cards for the people and their quotes.	20		
		Perform an infomercial that convinces others that science is either fair or not fair.	25		
Characteristics of Living Things		Make a windowpane that shares the seven characteristics of living things.	10		
		Design a brochure that tells how to determine if something is living or nonliving. Be sure to include examples to help with the trickier aspects.	15		
		Complete a Venn diagram in which you compare and contrast a robotic arm with a real arm. Be sure to include the characteristics of living things.	15		
		Assemble a scrapbook that shows examples of things that demonstrate at least three living characteristics but are not actually alive.	20		
Any		**Free choice**—Submit a proposal form to your teacher for a product of your choice.			
		Total number of points you are planning to earn.		**Total points earned:**	

I am planning to complete _____ activities that could earn up to a total of _____ points.

Teacher's initials _____ Student's signature _____

The Microscope

20-50-80 Menu

Objectives Covered Through These Menus and These Activities

- Students will recognize different types of microscopes.
- Students will identify the different parts of a microscope and how each contributes to its function.
- Students will demonstrate how to create a wet and dry mount.
- Students will share the history behind the development of the microscope.

Materials Needed by Students for Completion

- Poster board or large white paper
- Blank index cards (for trading cards)
- Large blank or lined index cards (for instruction cards)
- Aluminum foil (for quiz boards)
- Holiday lights (for quiz boards)
- Wires (for quiz boards)
- Materials for three-dimensional timelines
- Access to microscopes and materials for wet and dry mounts

Special Notes on the Use of This Menu

- This menu gives students an opportunity to create a quiz board. A student-friendly information sheet that offers the steps for constructing a quiz board is available at http://www.cesiscience.org/attachments/article/100/QuizBoardDirections.pdf.

Time Frame

- 1–2 weeks—Students are given a menu as the unit is started, and the teacher discusses all of the product options on the menu. As the different options are discussed, students will choose the activities they are most interested in completing so they meet their goal of 100 points. As the lessons progress, the teacher and students refer back to the menu options associated with the content being taught.
- 1–2 days—The teacher chooses an activity or product from the menu to use with the entire class.

Suggested Forms
- All-purpose rubric
- Student-taught lesson rubric
- Proposal form for point-based projects

Name:_____ Date:_____

The Microscope

Directions: Choose at least two activities from the menu below. The activities must total 100 points. Place a check mark next to each box to show which activities you will complete. All activities must be completed by _____.

---

20 Points

❏ Develop a set of trading cards for six different types of microscopes. Include at least two microscopes that do not use light and the various ways that they are used.

❏ Complete a Venn diagram to compare and contrast a compound microscope and a stereo microscope.

---

50 Points

❏ Create an instruction card that shares all of the steps you need to perform in order to use the microscopes in your classroom. Perform a demonstration that shares your steps.

❏ Build a quiz board that has users match parts of a picture or drawing of a microscope with their function.

❏ Make a three-dimensional timeline of the development of the first microscope.

❏ **Free choice**—Submit a proposal form to your teacher for a product of your choice.

---

80 Points

❏ Your school is getting ready to purchase new microscopes for the science department. Research the different types of microscopes on the market and determine which type would be best for your school. Create a poster to share the information about your choice of microscope, including how it works and why you feel it is the best. Include the cost and budget the school would need to have to purchase enough for your school.

❏ Design a student-taught lesson that shows your classmates how to create both a wet and dry mount as well as how to properly view each on a microscope.

Cell Specialization

20-50-80 Menu

Objectives Covered Through This Menu and These Activities
- Students will recognize the role biology plays in current events.
- Students will distinguish between different levels of organization within the biosphere.
- Students will classify cell organelles according to their contribution to overall cell functions.

Materials Needed by Students for Completion
- Poster board or large white paper
- Blank index cards (for trading cards and concentration cards)
- DVD or VHS recorder (for commercial and public service announcements)
- Recycled materials (for models or cross-cut diagrams)

Special Notes on the Use of This Menu
- This menu gives students the opportunity to create a commercial and a public service announcement. Although students enjoy producing their own videos, there often are difficulties obtaining the equipment and scheduling the use of a video recorder. These activities can be modified by allowing students to act out the commercial or public service announcement (like a play) or, if students have the technology, allowing them to produce a webcam version of their product.
- This menu asks students to use recycled materials to create their models or cross-cut diagrams. This does not mean only plastic and paper; instead, students should focus on using materials in new ways. It works well if a box is started for recycled contributions at the beginning of the school year. That way, students always have access to these types of materials.

Time Frame
- 1–2 weeks—Students are given a menu as the unit is started, and the teacher discusses all of the product options on the menu. As the different options are discussed, students will choose the activities they are most interested in completing so they meet their goal of 100

points. As the lessons progress, the teacher and students refer back to the menu options associated with the content being taught.
- 1–2 days—The teacher chooses an activity or product from the menu to use with the entire class.

Suggested Forms
- All-purpose rubric
- Proposal form for point-based projects

Name:_____ Date:_____

Cell Specialization

Directions: Choose at least two activities from the menu below. The activities must total 100 points. Place a check mark next to each box to show which activities you will complete. All activities must be completed by _____.

---

20 Points

❒ Make a levels of organization flipbook that has a flap for each level.

❒ Brainstorm multiple examples of each level of organization. Create a set of concentration cards for the examples and their respective levels.

---

50 Points

❒ Design a set of trading cards for 10 of the different types of specialized cells found in the human body.

❒ Not all organisms have specialized cells. Research one of these organisms and create a brochure that details the structure of the organism and how it carries out the functions that are usually associated with specialized cells.

❒ Write and perform a commercial for a specialized cell of your choice. Include why its unique function is so important to its organism.

❒ **Free choice**—Submit a proposal form to your teacher for a product of your choice.

---

80 Points

❒ Using recycled materials, build a model or cross-cut diagram of a specialized cell of your choice. Label all of the important organelles and structures and their special functions in the cell. Include a Venn diagram that compares and contrasts your specialized cell with a general cell's structure and organelles.

❒ There are various specialized cells in the human body. One of the most misunderstood is the fat cell. Record a public service announcement from the perspective of a fat cell about how it is specialized and why it plays an important part in the body's functions.

© Prufrock Press Inc. • *Differentiating Instruction With Menus: Biology* • *Grades 9–12*

Macromolecules

Game Show Menu

Objectives Covered Through This Menu and These Activities
- Students will recognize the role biology plays in current events.
- Students will analyze and interpret visual representations of biological processes.
- Students will identify the structure and function of macromolecules, including carbohydrates, nucleic acids, proteins, and lipids.

Materials Needed by Students for Completion
- Poster board or large white paper
- Magazines (for collages)
- Materials for board games (folders, colored cards, etc.)
- Recycled materials (for models)
- DVD or VHS recorder (for public service announcements and informational videos)
- Materials for three-dimensional timelines
- Internet access (for WebQuests)

Special Notes on the Use of This Menu
- This menu gives students the opportunity to create a public service announcement and an informational video. Although students enjoy producing their own videos, there often are difficulties obtaining the equipment and scheduling the use of a video recorder. This activity can be modified by allowing students to act out the public service announcement or informational video (like a play) or, if students have the technology, allowing them to produce a webcam version of their product.
- This menu asks students to use recycled materials to create their models. This does not mean only plastic and paper; instead, students should focus on using materials in new ways. It works well if a box is started for recycled contributions at the beginning of the school year. That way, students always have access to these types of materials.
- This menu gives students the opportunity to demonstrate a concept. This can take a significant amount of time and organization. It can save time if the demonstration is recorded to share at a later time or

if all of the students who choose to do a demonstration sign up for a designated day and time.

- This menu allows students to create a WebQuest. There are multiple versions and templates for WebQuests available on the Internet. Teachers should decide whether to specify a certain format or allow students to create one of their own choosing.

Time Frame

- 2–3 weeks—Students are given their menu as the unit is started and the guidelines and point expectations are discussed. As lessons are taught throughout the unit, students and the teacher can refer back to the options associated with that topic. The teacher will go over all of the options for the topic being covered and will have students place check marks in the boxes next to the activities they are most interested in completing. As teaching continues throughout the 2–3 weeks, activities are discussed, chosen, and submitted for grading.
- 1 week—At the beginning of the unit, the teacher chooses an activity from each area he or she feels would be most valuable for students. Stations can be set up in the classroom. These activities are available for student choice throughout the week as regular instruction takes place.
- 1–2 days—The teacher chooses an activity from an objective to use with the entire class during lesson time.

Suggested Forms

- All-purpose rubric
- Proposal form for point-based products

Guidelines for the Macromolecules Game Show Menu

- You must choose at least one activity from each topic area.
- You may not do more than two activities in any one topic area for credit. (You are, of course, welcome to do more than two for your own investigation.)
- Grading will be ongoing, so turn in products as you complete them.
- All free-choice proposals must be turned in and approved *prior* to working on a free-choice product.
- You must earn 100 points for a 100%. You may earn extra credit up to _____ points.
- You must show your teacher your plan for completion by: _____.

Name:_____ Date:_____

Macromolecules

Macromolecules	Carbohydrates	Nucleic Acids	Proteins	Lipids	Points for Each Level
☐ Draw a windowpane for the four types of macromolecules as well as the words monomer and polymer. (10 pts.)	☐ Construct a collage of different carbohydrates. Label each picture with its type of carbohydrate. Be sure you have examples from the different types! (10 pts.)	☐ Write three facts and a fib about the structure and importance of nucleic acids. (10 pts.)	☐ Make a folded quiz book about proteins, their structure, and peptide bonding. (10 pts.)	☐ Create a poster that shows the three types of lipids. Be sure to label the basic components. (10 pts.)	**10–15 points**
☐ Complete a Venn diagram to compare and contrast carbohydrates and lipids. (20 pts.)	☐ Design a mind map that shares the different kinds of carbohydrates, examples of each kind, and the important roles these molecules play in living things. (20 pts.)	☐ Develop a board game in which players answer questions about macromolecules and build their own nucleic acid as they proceed through the game. (25 pts.)	☐ Using recycled materials, create a model of a protein. Your protein should be able to show how it could become part of a polypeptide. Be sure your bonds are clearly visible and all particles are labeled. (20 pts.)	☐ Perform a demonstration to show how a triglyceride is formed. (20 pts.)	**20–25 points**
☐ There are certain processes and structures that are shared by all macromolecules. Create a WebQuest that has questors discovering how similar these macromolecules can be. Remember to go further than just their structure. (30 pts.)	☐ Write and perform a song that helps others understand how dehydration synthesis builds carbohydrates and remember the ratios of atoms in each type of carbohydrate because of this process. (30 pts.)	☐ Which nucleic acid came first? Determine the history behind the discovery of nucleic acids and their structure. Build a three-dimensional timeline sharing this information for the nucleic acid that was discovered first. (30 pts.)	☐ Select a protein you feel is most important to cellular function and create an informational video about why it is the most important and how the cells' functions would change without its presence. (30 pts.)	☐ Create a public service announcement that shares helpful information about the differences between the saturations of fat and which type is best for the body based on its structure. (30 pts.)	**30 points**
Free Choice (prior approval) (25–50 pts.)	**Free Choice** (prior approval) (25–50 pts.)	**Free Choice** (prior approval) (25–50 pts.)	**Free Choice** (prior approval) (25–50 pts.)	**Free Choice** (prior approval) (25–50 pts.)	**25–50 points**
Total:	Total:	Total:	Total:	Total:	Total Grade:

Plant and Animal Cells

20-50-80 Menu

Objectives Covered Through This Menu and These Activities

- Students will identify the basic structures and functions of plant and animal cells.
- Students will compare and contrast plant cells and animal cells including features that distinguish plant from animal cells.

Materials Needed by Students for Completion

- Poster board or large white paper
- Microsoft PowerPoint or other slideshow software
- Graph paper or Internet access (for crossword puzzles)
- Materials for board games (folders, colored cards, etc.)
- DVD or VHS recorder (for videos)
- Recycled materials (for models)

Special Notes on the Use of This Menu

- This menu gives students the opportunity to create a video. Although students enjoy producing their own videos, there often are difficulties obtaining the equipment and scheduling the use of a video recorder. This activity can be modified by allowing students to act out the video (like a play) or, if students have the technology, allowing them to produce a webcam version of their product.
- This menu asks students to use recycled materials to create their models. This does not mean only plastic and paper; instead, students should focus on using materials in new ways. It works well if a box is started for recycled contributions at the beginning of the school year. That way, students always have access to these types of materials.

Time Frame

- 1–2 weeks—Students are given a menu as the unit is started, and the teacher discusses all of the product options on the menu. As the different options are discussed, students will choose the activities they are most interested in completing so they meet their goal of 100 points. As the lessons progress, the teacher and students refer back to the menu options associated with the content being taught.

- 1–2 days—The teacher chooses an activity or product from the menu to use with the entire class.

Suggested Forms

- All-purpose rubric
- Proposal form for point-based projects

Plant and Animal Cells

Directions: Choose at least two activities from the menu below. The activities must total 100 points. Place a check mark next to each box to show which activities you will complete. All activities must be completed by _____.

---

20 Points

❏ Complete a Venn diagram flipbook that compares and contrasts all aspects of plant and animal cells, including structures and functions.

❏ Design a plant and animal cell crossword puzzle that focuses on the structural differences between the two types of cells.

---

50 Points

❏ Create a PowerPoint presentation quiz that your classmates could use to identify organelles in different photos of different types of plants and animal cells. Be creative in your labeling. Be sure to give credit for the photos you use!

❏ You have been hired by an educational network to create a television show. The topic of your first episode is plant and animal cells in our daily lives. Record a video of your first episode!

❏ Design a board game in which players are either a plant or animal cell traveling from organelle to organelle in the way that substances might move through one of these cells.

❏ **Free choice**—Submit a proposal form to your teacher for a product of your choice.

---

80 Points

❏ A plant cell and an animal cell are having a disagreement about which is the more complex cell. Write and present a play that shows their debate and concludes with who really is the most complex.

❏ There are structures that are found only in plant cells. Design a plant cell person that would represent how the human body would be different if it had the structures that plant cells contain. Build a model of your person using recycled objects with an accompanying poster that points out his or her important features.

CHAPTER 6

Classification of Organisms

```
20
  ☐
50
  ☐
  ☐
  ☐
80
  ☐
  ☐
```

Taxonomy

20-50-80 Menu

Objectives Covered Through This Menu and These Activities

- Students will identify traits of organisms within a species.
- Students will understand the major categories of biological classification.
- Students will recognize and use scientific names.
- Students will create a phylogenetic tree, cladogram, or dichotomous key.

Materials Needed by Students for Completion

- Poster board or large white paper
- Coat hangers (for mobiles)
- String (for mobiles)
- Blank index cards (for mobiles and card sorts)
- Large blank or lined index cards (for instruction cards)
- Materials for three-dimensional timelines

Special Notes on the Use of This Menu

- This menu gives students the opportunity to organize a class model. The expectation is that all students in the classroom will play an active role in the model. This may mean that the student designing the model may need some additional space for his or her model.

Time Frame

- 1–2 weeks—Students are given a menu as the unit is started, and the teacher discusses all of the product options on the menu. As the different options are discussed, students will choose the activities they are most interested in completing so they meet their goal of 100 points. As the lessons progress, the teacher and students refer back to the menu options associated with the content being taught.
- 1–2 days—The teacher chooses an activity or product from the menu to use with the entire class.

Suggested Forms

- All-purpose rubric
- Proposal form for point-based projects

Taxonomy

Directions: Choose at least two activities from the menu below. The activities must total 100 points. Place a check mark next to each box to show which activities you will complete. All activities must be completed by _____.

---

20 Points

❏ Create a mobile that shares the different taxonomy models that biologists have used to classify living things.

❏ Write an instruction card that explains how to create a dichotomous key, cladogram, or phylogenetic tree.

---

50 Points

❏ Create a three-dimensional timeline that shows how the classification of organisms has changed with different scientists' work.

❏ Facilitate a classroom model that will show how the classification of certain organisms would change based on which taxonomy model is used.

❏ Compare and contrast the benefits of two different taxonomy models using a Venn diagram.

❏ **Free choice**—Submit a proposal form to your teacher for a product of your choice.

---

80 Points

❏ Design a card sort that could be used to model the process biologists have gone through when they have tried to develop a taxonomy.

❏ Organisms are not the only things that can evolve. Using a popular line of toys, clothing, or cars, create a poster with a phylogenetic tree that shows how the product line you have chosen has changed over time, as well as its logical classification.

Comparing Different Organisms

20-50-80 Menu

Objectives Covered Through This Menu and These Activities

- Students will analyze and interpret visual representations of biological processes.
- Students will identify traits of organisms within a species.
- Students will demonstrate how the major categories of biological classification show that some organisms are more closely related than others.
- Students will recognize and use scientific names.
- Students will create a phylogenetic tree.

Materials Needed by Students for Completion

- Poster board or large white paper
- Recycled materials (for models)
- Large blank or lined index cards (for instruction cards)
- Scrapbooking materials

Special Notes on the Use of This Menu

- This menu asks students to use recycled materials to create their models. This does not mean only plastic and paper; instead, students should focus on using materials in new ways. It works well if a box is started for recycled contributions at the beginning of the school year. That way, students always have access to these types of materials.

Time Frame

- 1–2 weeks—Students are given a menu as the unit is started, and the teacher discusses all of the product options on the menu. As the different options are discussed, students will choose the activities they are most interested in completing so they meet their goal of 100 points. As the lessons progress, the teacher and students refer back to the menu options associated with the content being taught.
- 1–2 days—The teacher chooses an activity or product from the menu to use with the entire class.

Suggested Forms

- All-purpose rubric
- Student-taught lesson rubric
- Proposal form for point-based projects

Name:_____ Date:_____

Comparing Different Organisms

Directions: Choose at least two activities from the menu below. The activities must total 100 points. Place a check mark next to each box to show which activities you will complete. All activities must be completed by _____.

20 Points

- ☐ Make a flipbook with aspects that can be used to compare and contrast different organisms. Give an example of each.
- ☐ Design an instruction card that explains the steps a biologist would go through to determine how similar or different two organisms are.

50 Points

- ☐ Develop a three-item Venn diagram to compare and contrast three different organisms.
- ☐ Using recycled materials, build a model that can be used to demonstrate how similar or different two organisms are. Demonstrate these observations for your classmates.
- ☐ Select a feature or specific characteristic of living things that you find interesting. Make a scrapbook with organisms from different phyla and classes that have this trait in common. Be sure to indicate each organism's classification, and although they have the characteristic in common, share how each is different from the others included in your scrapbook.
- ☐ **Free choice**—Submit a proposal form to your teacher for a product of your choice.

80 Points

- ☐ Select two organisms that are not in the same classification class. Brainstorm a phylogenetic tree with at least 15 organisms, including the two you have chosen. Use the tree you have created to explain how these organisms are both similar and different. Create a poster that shows your phylogenetic tree and your basis of comparison.
- ☐ Prepare and present a class lesson that has students learn how organisms are alike and different. There should be at least one activity in the lesson in which students get to look at organisms, discuss them, and compare structures. Remember to submit your lesson ideas to your teacher for approval before your scheduled time!

Viruses

Tic-Tac-Toe Menu

Objectives Covered Through This Menu and These Activities

- Students will recognize the role biology plays in current events.
- Students will use the process of scientific reasoning to investigate scientific problems.
- Students will understand the characteristics of viruses and how they reproduce.
- Students will investigate different diseases that are caused by viruses.

Materials Needed by Students for Completion

- Poster board or large white paper
- Microsoft PowerPoint or other slideshow software
- DVD or VHS recorder (for news reports)
- Recycled materials (for models)

Special Notes on the Use of This Menu

- This menu gives students the opportunity to create a news report. Although students enjoy producing their own videos, there often are difficulties obtaining the equipment and scheduling the use of a video recorder. This activity can be modified by allowing students to act out the news report (like a play) or, if students have the technology, allowing them to produce a webcam version of their product.
- This menu asks students to use recycled materials to create their models. This does not mean only plastic and paper; instead, students should focus on using materials in new ways. It works well if a box is started for recycled contributions at the beginning of the school year. That way, students always have access to these types of materials.

Time Frame

- 2–3 weeks—Students are given the menu as the unit is started. As the teacher presents lessons throughout the week, he or she should refer back to the menu options associated with that content. The teacher will go over all of the options for that content and have students place check marks in the boxes that represent the activities they are most interested in completing. As students choose activities, they should complete a column or a row. When students complete this pattern, they have completed one activity from each content area, learning style, or level of Bloom's revised taxonomy, depending on the design of the menu.

- 1 week–At the start of the unit, the teacher chooses the three activities he or she feels are most valuable for students. Stations can be set up in the classroom. These three activities are available for student choice throughout the week as regular instruction takes place.
- 1–2 days—The teacher chooses an activity from the menu to use with the entire class.

Suggested Forms

- All-purpose rubric
- Free-choice proposal form

Name:_____ Date:_____

Viruses

Directions: Check the boxes you plan to complete. They should form a tic-tac-toe across or down. All activities must be completed by _____.

☐ *Structure of a Virus*	☐ *Research a Virus*	☐ *How Viruses Reproduce*
Make a flipbook with a virus drawn on the top. Cut the flipbook in such a way that each part of the virus is on a different flap. Record information about each structure inside each flap.	Select a disease that is caused by a virus and is still a problem for humans today. Research the virus that causes the disease, and produce a PowerPoint presentation to educate your classmates on the disease itself, the virus that causes it, how it is spread, and other important information.	Complete a Venn diagram to compare and contrast the different ways that viruses reproduce. Include examples of each type in your diagram.
☐ *How Viruses Reproduce*	☐ **Free Choice on the Structure of Viruses** *(Fill out your proposal form before beginning the free choice!)*	☐ *Research a Virus*
Create a folded quiz book about the ways in which viruses reproduce. Be sure to include drawings in your quiz.		Research a disease that is caused by a retrovirus. Perform a news report about the disease and its virus. Include how this type of virus is different, how it replicates, how it is spread, and what is being done about the disease.
☐ *Research a Virus*	☐ *How Viruses Reproduce*	☐ *Structure of a Virus*
Research a viral disease that is being successfully controlled through vaccination. Come to class as the scientist who had the greatest impact on the vaccination. Share information about the virus, how it spreads, and how the vaccine works.	It has been said that at any moment, there are viruses in your body even though you do not feel sick. Write a children's book that proves whether this statement is true or false.	Build a model of a virus using recycled materials that you can find at home. Label all of the important structures on your model and include at least two sentences about how the structure impacts the function of the virus.

The Five Kingdoms

Game Show Menu

Objectives Covered Through This Menu and These Activities

- Students will recognize the role biology plays in current events.
- Students will analyze and interpret visual representations of biological processes.
- Students will distinguish between different levels of organization within the biosphere.
- Students will identify traits of organisms within a species.
- Students will demonstrate how the major categories of biological classification show that some organisms are more closely related than others.
- Students will recognize and use scientific names.
- Students will identify examples of biodiversity at the ecosystem level.

Materials Needed by Students for Completion

- Poster board or large white paper
- Magazines (for collages)
- Microsoft PowerPoint or other slideshow software
- DVD or VHS recorder (for videos)
- Scrapbooking materials
- Aluminum foil (for quiz boards)
- Holiday lights (for quiz boards)
- Wires (for quiz boards)
- Materials for three-dimensional timelines
- Materials for MIPP trophy
- Internet access (for WebQuests)

Special Notes on the Use of This Menu

- This menu gives students the opportunity to create a video. Although students enjoy producing their own videos, there often are difficulties obtaining the equipment and scheduling the use of a video recorder. This activity can be modified by allowing students to act out the video (like a play) or, if students have the technology, allowing them to produce a webcam version of their product.
- This menu gives students an opportunity to create a quiz board. A student-friendly information sheet that offers the steps for constructing

a quiz board is available at http://www.cesiscience.org/attachments/article/100/QuizBoardDirections.pdf.

- This menu allows students to create a WebQuest. There are multiple versions and templates for WebQuests available on the Internet. Teachers should decide whether to specify a certain format or allow students to create one of their own choosing.

Time Frame

- 2–3 weeks—Students are given their menu as the unit is started and the guidelines and point expectations are discussed. As lessons are taught throughout the unit, students and the teacher can refer back to the options associated with that topic. The teacher will go over all of the options for the topic being covered and will have students place check marks in the boxes next to the activities they are most interested in completing. As teaching continues throughout the 2–3 weeks, activities are discussed, chosen, and submitted for grading.
- 1 week—At the beginning of the unit, the teacher chooses an activity from each area he or she feels would be most valuable for students. Stations can be set up in the classroom. These activities are available for student choice throughout the week as regular instruction takes place.
- 1–2 days—The teacher chooses an activity from an objective to use with the entire class during lesson time.

Suggested Forms

- All-purpose rubric
- Student-taught lesson rubric
- Proposal form for point-based products

Guidelines for The Five Kingdoms Game Show Menu

- You must choose at least one activity from each topic area.
- You may not do more than two activities in any one topic area for credit. (You are, of course, welcome to do more than two for your own investigation.)
- Grading will be ongoing, so turn in products as you complete them.
- All free-choice proposals must be turned in and approved *prior* to working on a free-choice product.
- You must earn 110 points for a 100%. You may earn extra credit up to _____ points.
- You must show your teacher your plan for completion by: _____.

The Five Kingdoms

The Kingdom Monera	The Kingdom Protista	The Kingdom Fungi	The Kingdom Plantae	The Kingdom Animalia	Points for Each Level
☐ Write an acrostic for the word *Monera*. Include specific characteristics about this kingdom for each letter. (10 pts.)	☐ Design a flipbook that shares the unique features of the Kingdom Protista. (10 pts.)	☐ Build a quiz board to test others on the structures found within all fungi. (15 pts.)	☐ Create a collage of interesting plants and label the phyla for each. (10 pts.)	☐ Make a mind map to show the Kingdom Animalia and its phyla. Include at least one basic yet unique trait for each phylum. (15 pts.)	**10–15 points**
☐ Prepare a three-dimensional geological timeline that shows when monerans first appeared in Earth's history as well as how they have changed to present day. (20 pts.)	☐ Some people say that the organisms classified as protists are classified this way because they do not belong in any other kingdom. Create a children's book about a protist that is trying to find its proper classification. (25 pts.)	☐ Design a scrapbook for the Kingdom Fungi that focuses on the biodiversity of organisms within the kingdom. (20 pts.)	☐ Complete a Venn diagram to compare and contrast two different phyla within the Kingdom Plantae. (20 pts.)	☐ Select one characteristic of living things and trace it through all of the phyla in this kingdom. Prepare a PowerPoint presentation that shows what you discovered through pictures. (25 pts.)	**20–25 points**
☐ Keep a diary or journal for 12 hours in the life of a monera that is important to humans. Include entries that describe its internal functions and how it responds to the environment. (30 pts.)	☐ If there was a Most Important Protist to People (MIPP) award, which organism from this kingdom should receive it? Create a trophy for the award and a nomination letter for the protist you believe should win. (30 pts.)	☐ Present a student-taught lesson on fungi, their structures, and their benefits to us in our daily lives. (30 pts.)	☐ Perform a skit (or make a video) in which a nonvascular plant of your choice is interviewing a Sequoia about what it takes to make it to such great heights. (30 pts.)	☐ Design a WebQuest that shows examples of how the complexity changes across the phyla in this kingdom. (30 pts.)	**30 points**
Free Choice (prior approval) (25–50 pts.)	**Free Choice** (prior approval) (25–50 pts.)	**Free Choice** (prior approval) (25–50 pts.)	**Free Choice** (prior approval) (25–50 pts.)	**Free Choice** (prior approval) (25–50 pts.)	**25–50 points**
Total:	Total:	Total:	Total:	Total:	Total: Grade:

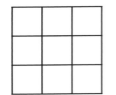

The Kingdom Monera

Tic-Tac-Toe Menu

Objectives Covered Through This Menu and These Activities

- Students will recognize the role biology plays in current events.
- Students will analyze and interpret visual representations of biological processes.
- Students will recognize the role biology plays in current events.
- Students will identify traits of organisms within the Kingdom Monera.
- Students will recognize and use scientific names.
- Students will identify examples of biodiversity within the Kingdom Monera.
- Students will recognize basic structures and functions within the Kingdom Monera.

Materials Needed by Students for Completion

- Poster board or large white paper
- Blank index cards (for trading cards)
- Materials for three-dimensional timelines
- Scrapbooking materials
- Graph paper or Internet access (for crossword puzzles)
- Aluminum foil (for quiz boards)
- Holiday lights (for quiz boards)
- Wires (for quiz boards)
- Newspapers or access to online newspapers
- DVD or VHS recorder (for commercials and news reports)

Special Notes on the Use of This Menu

- This menu gives students the opportunity to create a commercial and a news report. Although students enjoy producing their own videos, there often are difficulties obtaining the equipment and scheduling the use of a video recorder. This activity can be modified by allowing students to act out the commercial or news report (like a play) or, if students have the technology, allowing them to produce a webcam version of their product.
- This menu gives students an opportunity to create a quiz board. A student-friendly information sheet that offers the steps for constructing

a quiz board is available at http://www.cesiscience.org/attachments/
article/100/QuizBoardDirections.pdf.

Time Frame

- 2–3 weeks—Students are given the menu as the unit is started. As the teacher presents lessons throughout the week, he or she should refer back to the menu options associated with that content. The teacher will go over all of the options for that content and have students place check marks in the boxes that represent the activities they are most interested in completing. As students choose activities, they should complete a column or a row. When students complete this pattern, they have completed one activity from each content area, learning style, or level of Bloom's revised taxonomy, depending on the design of the menu.
- 1 week—At the start of the unit, the teacher chooses the three activities he or she feels are most valuable for students. Stations can be set up in the classroom. These three activities are available for student choice throughout the week as regular instruction takes place.
- 1–2 days—The teacher chooses an activity from the menu to use with the entire class.

Suggested Forms

- All-purpose rubric
- Free-choice proposal form

Name:_____ Date:_____

The Kingdom Monera

Directions: Check the boxes you plan to complete. They should form a tic-tac-toe across or down. All products are due by: _____.

☐ *Structure and Function*	☐ *Moneran Organisms*	☐ *Everyday Monerans*
Build a quiz board to quiz users on the names and functions of the various structures found in the Kingdom Monera.	Design a three-dimensional geological timeline that shows when monerans first appeared and how they have changed to present day. Be sure to include examples of and reasons for the various changes monerans have experienced on your timeline.	Make a Kingdom Monera scrapbook that shares pictures of various monerans we experience on a daily basis. Focus on the diversity of the kingdom as well as the degree of complexity. Label similar structures in each picture and share their importance to the organism's survival.
☐ *Everyday Monerans*	☐ **Free Choice on the Structure and Function of Organisms in the Kingdom Monera** (Fill out your proposal form before beginning the free choice!)	☐ *Moneran Organisms*
Find a newspaper article that discusses the impact that an organism from the Kingdom Monera is having on your community. Use the information in the article to create a news report about what is happening and provide some solutions to the problem.		Design a crossword puzzle that asks about common monerans, their structures, and the valuable functions they serve in our environment.
☐ *Moneran Organisms*	☐ *Everyday Monerans*	☐ *Structure and Function*
Develop a set of trading cards for various types of bacteria found within this kingdom. In addition to the standard information, include what makes the organism unique and interesting on your cards.	Keep a diary or journal for 24 hours in the life of your favorite moneran. Include entries that describe its internal functions as well as how it responds to the environment.	Is being unicellular such a bad thing? Record a commercial in which a moneran tries to convince watchers that being unicellular is actually the best way to be!

```
20
  ❑
  ❑
50
  ❑
  ❑
  ❑
  ❑
80
  ❑
  ❑
```

The Kingdom Protista

20-50-80 Menu

Objectives Covered Through This Menu and These Activities
- Students will analyze and interpret visual representations of biological processes.
- Students will recognize the role biology plays in current events.
- Students will identify traits of organisms within the Kingdom Protista.
- Students will recognize and use scientific names.
- Students will identify examples of biodiversity within the Kingdom Protista.
- Students will recognize basic structures and functions within the Kingdom Protista.

Materials Needed by Students for Completion
- Poster board or large white paper
- Blank index cards (for card sorts)
- Materials for bulletin board displays
- Internet access (for WebQuests)

Special Notes on the Use of This Menu
- This menu allows students to create a bulletin board display. Some classrooms may only have one bulletin board, so the teacher can divide the board into sections, or additional classroom wall or hall space can be sectioned off for the creation of these displays. Students can plan their display based on the amount of space they are assigned.
- This menu allows students to create a WebQuest. There are multiple versions and templates for WebQuests available on the Internet. Teachers should decide whether to specify a certain format or allow students to create one of their own choosing.

Time Frame
- 1–2 weeks—Students are given a menu as the unit is started, and the teacher discusses all of the product options on the menu. As the different options are discussed, students will choose the activities they are most interested in completing so they meet their goal of 100 points. As the lessons progress, the teacher and students refer back to the menu options associated with the content being taught.

- 1–2 days—The teacher chooses an activity or product from the menu to use with the entire class.

Suggested Forms
- All-purpose rubric
- Proposal form for point-based projects

The Kingdom Protista

Directions: Choose at least two activities from the menu below. The activities must total 100 points. Place a check mark next to each box to show which activities you will complete. All activities must be completed by _____.

---

20 Points

❐ Create a card sort that could be used to tell whether or not an organism belongs in the Kingdom Protista.

❐ Design a flipbook that shares the unique features of the Kingdom Protista.

---

50 Points

❐ Select a simple and a more complex protist. Complete a Venn diagram to compare and contrast these two organisms.

❐ Protists participate in symbiotic relationships with other organisms. Prepare a bulletin board display that shows specific examples of these relationships between protists and other organisms.

❐ Write and perform a song about what is special about a protist's way of life.

❐ **Free choice**—Submit a proposal form to your teacher for a product of your choice.

---

80 Points

❐ Some people say that the organisms classified as protists are classified this way because they do not belong in any other kingdom. What do you think? Create a children's book about a protist that is trying to find its proper classification.

❐ Develop a Kingdom Protista WebQuest that has questors visit informational websites that include videos with different examples of protists. In addition to the structures and characteristics of the different protists, include information on how this kingdom has changed over time.

```
20
  ❑
  ❑
50
  ❑
  ❑
  ❑
  ❑
80
  ❑
  ❑
```

The Kingdom Fungi

20-50-80 Menu

Objectives Covered Through This Menu and These Activities

- Students will recognize the role biology plays in current events.
- Students will identify traits of organisms within the Kingdom Fungi.
- Students will recognize and use scientific names.
- Students will identify examples of biodiversity within the Kingdom Fungi.
- Students will recognize basic structures and functions within the Kingdom Fungi.

Materials Needed by Students for Completion

- Poster board or large white paper
- Large blank or lined index cards (for recipe cards)
- Blank index cards (for trading cards)
- Scrapbooking materials
- DVD or VHS recorder (for videos)

Special Notes on the Use of This Menu

- This menu gives students the opportunity to create a video. Although students enjoy producing their own videos, there often are difficulties obtaining the equipment and scheduling the use of a video recorder. This activity can be modified by allowing students to act out the video (like a play) or, if students have the technology, allowing them to produce a webcam version of their product.

Time Frame

- 1–2 weeks—Students are given a menu as the unit is started, and the teacher discusses all of the product options on the menu. As the different options are discussed, students will choose the activities they are most interested in completing so they meet their goal of 100 points. As the lessons progress, the teacher and students refer back to the menu options associated with the content being taught.
- 1–2 days—The teacher chooses an activity or product from the menu to use with the entire class.

Suggested Forms

- All-purpose rubric
- Proposal form for point-based projects

Name:_____ Date:_____

The Kingdom Fungi

Directions: Choose at least two activities from the menu below. The activities must total 100 points. Place a check mark next to each box to show which activities you will complete. All activities must be completed by _____.

---

20 Points

❏ Create a flipbook of characteristics of the organisms within the Kingdom Fungi. Name each characteristic on the top flap and then draw and name a specific example for each.

❏ Write a recipe card that could be used to create an organism that would be classified in the Kingdom Fungi.

---

50 Points

❏ Create a set of trading cards for the different phyla of Fungi. Be sure to include the traits that differentiate one phylum from another.

❏ Write and perform a song to teach others about the special structures and functions that make the Kingdom Fungi so unique.

❏ Design a scrapbook for the Kingdom Fungi that focuses on the biodiversity of organisms within the kingdom.

❏ **Free choice**—Submit a proposal form to your teacher for a product of your choice.

---

80 Points

❏ Organisms within the Kingdom Fungi play very important roles in their environment. Select an organism from this kingdom and perform a "You Be the Fungi" presentation in which you discuss your importance in the environment. Be as specific as you can be!

❏ Fungi are often misunderstood and considered a nuisance. Develop and record an educational video called "Fungi Are Our Friends." (You may select another title if you prefer.) Your video should share important information about the Kingdom Fungi and how it impacts our lives.

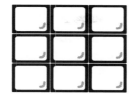

The Kingdom Plantae

Game Show Menu

Objectives Covered Through This Menu and These Activities
- Students will recognize the role biology plays in current events.
- Students will identify traits of organisms within the Kingdom Plantae, specifically the characteristics of nonvascular plants, seedless vascular plants, gymnosperms, and angiosperms.
- Students will recognize and use scientific names.
- Students will identify examples of biodiversity within the Kingdom Plantae.

Materials Needed by Students for Completion
- Poster board or large white paper
- Blank index cards (for trading cards)
- Recycled materials (for cross-cut models)
- Scrapbooking materials
- Materials for MIPP trophy

Special Notes on the Use of This Menu
- This menu asks students to use recycled materials to create their cross-cut models. This does not mean only plastic and paper; instead, students should focus on using materials in new ways. It works well if a box is started for recycled contributions at the beginning of the school year. That way, students always have access to these types of materials.
- This menu gives students the opportunity to demonstrate a concept. This can take a significant amount of time and organization. It can save time if the demonstration is recorded to share at a later time or if all of the students who choose to do a demonstration sign up for a designated day and time.

Time Frame
- 2–3 weeks—Students are given their menu as the unit is started and the guidelines and point expectations are discussed. As lessons are taught throughout the unit, students and the teacher can refer back to the options associated with that topic. The teacher will go over all of the options for the topic being covered and will have students

place check marks in the boxes next to the activities they are most interested in completing. As teaching continues throughout the 2–3 weeks, activities are discussed, chosen, and submitted for grading.

- 1 week—At the beginning of the unit, the teacher chooses an activity from each area he or she feels would be most valuable for students. Stations can be set up in the classroom. These activities are available for student choice throughout the week as regular instruction takes place.
- 1–2 days—The teacher chooses an activity from an objective to use with the entire class during lesson time.

Suggested Forms

- All-purpose rubric
- Student-taught lesson rubric
- Proposal form for point-based products

Guidelines for The Kingdom Plantae Game Show Menu

- You must choose at least one activity from each topic area.
- You may not do more than two activities in any one topic area for credit. (You are, of course, welcome to do more than two for your own investigation.)
- Grading will be ongoing, so turn in products as you complete them.
- All free-choice proposals must be turned in and approved *prior* to working on a free-choice product.
- You must earn 120 points for a 100%. You may earn extra credit up to _____ points.
- You must show your teacher your plan for completion by: _____.

The Kingdom Plantae

Name:_____ Date:_____

Nonvascular Plants	Seedless Vascular Plants	Gymnosperms	Angiosperms	Kingdom Plantae and You	Points for Each Level
☐ Draw a windowpane with at least six examples of nonvascular plants that can be found locally. (10 pts.)	☐ Create a folded quiz book about what makes these plants deserve their own spot in the Plantae Kingdom. (10 pts.)	☐ Make a set of trading cards for the different gymnosperms that are found in your area. (15 pts.)	☐ Using recycled materials, build a cross-cut model of an angiosperm. Label all of the structures and include the function of each. (15 pts.)	☐ Design a poster that shows various ways in which all of these types of plants are used in our lives. (15 pts.)	10–15 points
☐ Create an advertisement that focuses on the specialized structures of nonvascular plants. (20 pts.)	☐ Because these plants do not contain seeds, perform a demonstration for your classmates that shows how these plants reproduce. (25 pts.)	☐ A new nonfiction book has been written about gymnosperms and what makes them different from angiosperms. Create a book cover for this new book. (20 pts.)	☐ Write and perform a song to help your classmates remember the different structures commonly found in angiosperms. (20 pts.)	☐ Develop a class game to test your classmates' knowledge about how different types of plants are used in food, medicine, and manufacturing. (25 pts.)	20–25 points
☐ If a nonvascular plant could change one thing about itself, what would it be? Perform a play about a nonvascular plant that is just not happy with one of its structures or functions. (30 pts.)	☐ Present a student-taught lesson on seedless vascular plants. Focus on more than just their structures—include their uses in our everyday lives. (30 pts.)	☐ Perform a persuasive speech to convince others that although it may not seem obvious, these phyla play an important role in our environment. (30 pts.)	☐ Make an angiosperm scrapbook in which you collect leaves and/or flowers from locally growing angiosperms. After pressing all your samples, identify each in your scrapbook. (30 pts.)	☐ If there was a Most Important Plant to People (MIPP) award, which organism from this kingdom should receive it? Create a trophy for the award and a nomination letter for the plant you believe should win. (30 pts.)	30 points
Free Choice (prior approval) (25–50 pts.)	**Free Choice** (prior approval) (25–50 pts.)	**Free Choice** (prior approval) (25–50 pts.)	**Free Choice** (prior approval) (25–50 pts.)	**Free Choice** (prior approval) (25–50 pts.)	25–50 points
Total:	Total:	Total:	Total:	Total:	Total Grade:

92   © Prufrock Press Inc. • *Differentiating Instruction With Menus: Biology • Grades 9–12*

The Kingdom Animalia

Meal Menu

Objectives Covered Through This Menu and These Activities

- Students will recognize how the Kingdom Animalia is distributed.
- Students will identify traits of organisms within the Kingdom Animalia.
- Students will recognize and use scientific names.
- Students will identify examples of biodiversity within the Kingdom Animalia.
- Students will recognize basic structures and functions within the Kingdom Animalia.
- Students will create a dichotomous key, phylogenetic tree, or cladogram.

Materials Needed by Students for Completion

- Poster board or large white paper
- Blank index cards (for card sort games)
- Materials for bulletin board displays
- Microsoft PowerPoint or other slideshow software
- DVD or VHS recorder (for educational videos)

Special Notes on the Use of This Menu

- This menu gives students the opportunity to create an educational video. Although students enjoy producing their own videos, there often are difficulties obtaining the equipment and scheduling the use of a video recorder. This activity can be modified by allowing students to act out the video (like a play) or, if students have the technology, allowing them to produce a webcam version of their product.
- This menu allows students to create a bulletin board display. Some classrooms may only have one bulletin board, so the teacher can divide the board into sections, or additional classroom wall or hall space can be sectioned off for the creation of these displays. Students can plan their display based on the amount of space they are assigned.

Time Frame

- 1–3 weeks—Students are given the menu as the unit is started. As the lesson or unit progresses throughout the week, students should refer back to the menu options associated with that content. The teacher will go over all of the options for that content and have students place a check mark in the box for each option that represents the activity they are most interested in completing. As teaching continues, the activities chosen and completed should create a full day's meal, with a breakfast, a lunch, a dinner, and an optional dessert. The teacher may choose to allow students time to work after other work is finished. When students complete the menu with this expectation, they have completed one activity from each content area, learning style, or level of Bloom's revised taxonomy, depending on the design of the menu.

- 1–2 days—The teacher chooses an activity or product from an objective to use with the entire class during that lesson time.

Suggested Forms

- All-purpose rubric
- Free-choice proposal form

Name:_____ Date:_____

The Kingdom Animalia

Directions: You must choose one activity each for breakfast, lunch, and dinner. Dessert is an activity you can choose to do after you have finished your other meals. All products must be completed by: _____.

Breakfast

❑ Make a mind map to show how the Kingdom Animalia is divided into phyla and the basic traits of these phyla.

❑ Create a bulletin board display that shows the general distribution of organisms within the Kingdom Animalia.

❑ Write and perform a song about the characteristics of organisms within the Kingdom Animalia.

Lunch

❑ Select two phyla in this kingdom and complete a Venn diagram to compare and contrast the characteristics of the organisms in each.

❑ There is one main separation within the Kingdom Animalia. Create a card sort game that has users determining where specialized structures, specific functions, and certain organisms would be classified.

❑ Using a poster, design a dichotomous key, a phylogenetic tree, or a cladogram that includes at least two phyla in the Kingdom Animalia.

Dinner

❑ Design a PowerPoint presentation that shows examples of how the complexity changes across the phyla in this kingdom.

❑ Select one characteristic of living things and trace it through all of the phyla in this kingdom. Make a mural that shows what you discovered.

❑ Write a children's book in which a sponge compares its characteristics of life with other organisms in its kingdom.

Dessert

❑ Record an educational video in which you share little-known facts about organisms within the various phyla in this kingdom.

❑ **Free choice**—Submit a proposal form to your teacher for a product of your choice about the Kingdom Animalia.

The Human Body

Baseball Menu

Objectives Covered Through This Menu and These Activities

- Students will understand the structure and function of the organs and organs systems within the human body, including the digestive, circulatory, skeletal, respiratory, muscular, nervous, endocrine, execratory, integumentary, and immune systems.
- Students will communicate the interdependence between the different systems.
- Students will recognize the role biology plays in current events.
- Students will analyze and interpret visual representations of biological processes.

Materials Needed by Students for Completion

- Poster board or large white paper
- Blank index cards (for mobiles, trading cards, and concentration cards)
- Coat hangers (for mobiles)
- String (for mobiles)
- Materials for board games (folders, colored cards, etc.)
- Recycled materials (for models)
- Internet access (for WebQuests)
- DVD or VHS recorder (for videos)

Special Notes on the Use of This Menu

- This menu gives students the opportunity to create a video. Although students enjoy producing their own videos, there often are difficulties obtaining the equipment and scheduling the use of a video recorder. This activity can be modified by allowing students to act out the video (like a play) or, if students have the technology, allowing them to produce a webcam version of their product.
- This menu asks students to use recycled materials to create their models. This does not mean only plastic and paper; instead, students should focus on using materials in new ways. It works well if a box is started for recycled contributions at the beginning of the school year. That way, students always have access to these types of materials.

- This menu allows students to create a WebQuest. There are multiple versions and templates for WebQuests available on the Internet. Teachers should decide whether to specify a certain format or allow students to create one of their own choosing.

Time Frame

- 2–3 weeks—Students are given the menu as the unit is started, and the guidelines and point expectations are discussed. Students are expected to complete enough points to equal one run (100 points). Because this menu covers one topic in depth, the teacher will go over all of the options for the topic being covered and have students place check marks in the boxes next to the activities they are most interested in completing. As instruction continues, activities are completed by students and submitted for grading.
- 1 week—At the beginning of the unit, the teacher chooses one or two higher level activities that can be integrated into whole-group instruction throughout the week.
- 1–2 days—The teacher chooses an activity from an objective to use with the entire class during that lesson time.

Suggested Forms

- All-purpose rubric
- Proposal form for point-based projects

Name:_____   Date:_____

The Human Body

Directions: Look through the following choices and decide how you want to make your game add up to 100 points. Singles are worth 10, doubles are worth 30, triples are worth 50, and a home run is worth 100. Choose any combination you want. Place a check mark next to each choice you are going to complete. Make sure that your points equal 100!

These choices are not specific to any one body system. When you decide on your choices, plan on including all of the following systems in your products. For example, if you complete a product that compares two systems, then you have completed two systems. Mark them off as you complete them.

❒ Digestive System   ❒ Respiratory System   ❒ Endocrine System   ❒ Integumentary
❒ Circulatory System   ❒ Muscular System   ❒ Excretory System   System
❒ Skeletal System   ❒ Nervous System   ❒ Immune System

Singles—10 Points Each

❒ Make a mobile for a body system with all of its organs and their functions; include at least one additional system that is impacted by the body system you have selected.

❒ Create a mind map that shares information on two of the body systems.

❒ Design an acrostic for your body system. Provide descriptions about the function of the system for each letter.

❒ Develop a set of concentration cards to match organs in your system with the function they provide for the body.

❒ Write three facts and a fib about an organ in your body system.

❒ **Free choice**—Submit a proposal form to your teacher for a product of your choice.

Doubles—30 Points Each

❒ Design a set of trading cards for the organs within a body system of your choice. Each card should include how the organ's cells within that system are specialized to their function.

❒ Write a body system dictionary for two body systems. It should include all of the specialized vocabulary for each organ within the system.

❒ Make a human body board game. It must ask players to share information about at least four of the body systems.

❒ Using recycled materials, build a model of a body system that shows all of the organs. Include labels to share the functions of each organ.

❒ Develop an advertisement for a body system. Focus on the importance of the system.

The Human Body, *continued*

Triples—50 Points Each

- ❑ Although all of the systems of the human body are interdependent, which system do you feel is most important to the overall health of the body? Prepare a persuasive speech that explains your point of view.

- ❑ Keep a diary for a day in the life of a body system of your choice. Your day should begin when the body goes to sleep and continue for 24 hours. Be as specific as possible and be sure to include interactions with other organs and systems.

- ❑ Choose a body system that is not well known by primary children. Write a children's book that explains this system as well as how the other body systems rely on the body system you have selected.

- ❑ Investigate which body system seems to be most susceptible to disease. Create a WebQuest in which questors visit different websites to gather information on how diseases can affect each organ in the body system you have selected.

Homerun—100 Points

- ❑ You have been invited to be the first news reporter to participate in a new nanotechnology that allows people to shrink to super small sizes. In your smaller state, you will be able to travel through the human body, making various stops at organ systems and their organs. Use this opportunity to:

  - Interview all of the organs about their specialized cells (and terminology).
  - Inquire how each body system impacts the total health of the body.
  - Speak with at least one organ that is not functioning at its full potential (or may be diseased) and offer some advice to help this organ before proceeding on your trip.

  After deciding the order of your trip and how you would like it to be organized, create a video to document your trip through the body.

I Chose:

_____ Singles (10 points each)

_____ Doubles (30 points each)

_____ Triples (50 points each)

_____ Home Run (100 points)

CHAPTER 7

Heredity

DNA and RNA

Three-Topic List Menu

Objectives Covered Through This Menu and These Activities
- Students will explain the unique structures of DNA and RNA.
- Students will compare and contrast the structure and function of DNA and RNA.
- Students will research the discovery of DNA.
- Students will investigate real-world uses of DNA and RNA.

Materials Needed by Students for Completion
- Poster board or large white paper
- Recycled materials (for models)
- Ruler (for comic strips)
- Microsoft PowerPoint or other slideshow software
- DVD or VHS recorder (for infomercials)
- Materials for three-dimensional timelines
- Newspapers or access to online newspapers

Special Notes on the Use of This Menu
- This menu gives students the opportunity to create an infomercial. Although students enjoy producing their own videos, there often are difficulties obtaining the equipment and scheduling the use of a video recorder. This activity can be modified by allowing students to act out the infomercial (like a play) or, if students have the technology, allowing them to produce a webcam version of their product.
- This menu asks students to use recycled materials to create their models. This does not mean only plastic and paper; instead, students should focus on using materials in new ways. It works well if a box is started for recycled contributions at the beginning of the school year. That way, students always have access to these types of materials.
- This menu gives students the opportunity to organize a class model. The expectation is that all students in the classroom will play an active role in the model. This may mean that the student designing the model may need some additional space for his or her model.

Time Frame
- 1–2 weeks—Students are given the menu as the unit is started, and the guidelines and point expectations are discussed. Students will need to earn 100 points for 100%, although there is an opportunity for extra credit if the teacher would like to use another target number. Because this menu covers three topics in depth, the teacher may choose to only go over the options for the topic being covered first; the students place check marks in the boxes next to the activities they are most interested in completing. As instruction continues, additional explanation of the new topic activities can be provided. Once students have access to the entire menu, teachers will need to set aside a few moments to sign the agreement at the bottom of the page with each student. As students complete activities, they will be submitted to the teacher for grading.
- 1–2 days—The teacher chooses an activity or product from an objective to use with the entire class during that lesson time.

Suggested Forms
- All-purpose rubric
- Proposal form for point-based products

Name:_____ Date:_____

DNA and RNA

Guidelines:

1. You may complete as many of the activities listed as you can within the time period.
2. You may choose any combination of activities, but you **must** complete at least one activity from each topic area.
3. Your goal is 100 points. You may earn up to _____ points extra credit.
4. You may be as creative as you like within the guidelines listed below.
5. You must share your plan with your teacher by _____.
6. Activities may be turned in at any time during the working time period. They will be graded and recorded on this sheet as you continue to work, so keep it safe!

Topic	Plan to Do	Activity to Complete	Point Value	Date Completed	Points Earned
Structure of DNA		Make a flipbook that shows how the bases "match up" in the DNA molecule.	5		
		Consider the full name of DNA. Using your knowledge of biochemistry, create a poster to share how it got its name.	15		
		Perform an educational song to teach others about the structure of a DNA molecule.	20		
		Using recycled materials, build a model to show DNA's structure.	20		
		Design a class model that shows DNA's structure. Be sure to include at least one of each nitrogenous base.	25		
Comparing RNA and DNA		Complete a Venn diagram to compare and contrast DNA and RNA.	15		
		Design a folded quiz book that asks questions about DNA and RNA. No more than two questions can be about their structures.	20		
		Investigate why RNA must have the structure it has in order to complete its functions. Create an advertisement to showcase how its structure has benefits over DNA's structure.	20		
		Draw a comic strip in which DNA and RNA are arguing about who is most important.	25		
Real-World Application		Build a three-dimensional timeline for the discovery of DNA.	20		
		Find a newspaper article in which DNA plays a significant role. Write an analysis paragraph of the article.	20		
		Researchers have been investigating DNA for many years. Select one research project that has taken place within the last 2 years and create a PowerPoint presentation to share what is being studied and the findings so far.	25		
		GMOs have gained a lot of media attention recently. What is a GMO, and how does DNA and/or RNA play into the creation of GMOs? Perform an infomercial supporting or refuting their development.	30		
Any		**Free choice**—Submit a proposal form to your teacher for a product of your choice.			
		Total number of points you are planning to earn.		**Total points earned:**	

I am planning to complete _____ activities that could earn up to a total of _____ points.

Teacher's initials _____ Student's signature _____

© Prufrock Press Inc. • *Differentiating Instruction With Menus: Biology • Grades 9–12*

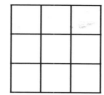

Mitosis and Meiosis

Tic-Tac-Toe Menu

Objectives Covered Through This Menu and These Activities

- Students will compare and contrast the processes of mitosis and meiosis.
- Students will understand what takes place during the various stages of mitosis and meiosis.
- Students will explain how meiosis results in sex cells.
- Students will identify the basic structures and explain the functions that allow an organism to pass on genetic information to its offspring.

Materials Needed by Students for Completion

- Poster board or large white paper
- Materials for board games (folders, colored cards, etc.)
- Ruler (for comic strips)

Special Notes on the Use of This Menu

- This menu gives students the opportunity to organize a class model. The expectation is that all students in the classroom will play an active role in the model. This may mean that the student designing the model may need some additional space for his or her model.

Time Frame

- 2–3 weeks—Students are given the menu as the unit is started. As the teacher presents lessons throughout the week, he or she should refer back to the menu options associated with that content. The teacher will go over all of the options for that content and have students place check marks in the boxes that represent the activities they are most interested in completing. As students choose activities, they should complete a column or a row. When students complete this pattern, they have completed one activity from each content area, learning style, or level of Bloom's revised taxonomy, depending on the design of the menu.
- 1 week—At the start of the unit, the teacher chooses the three activities he or she feels are most valuable for students. Stations can be set up in the classroom. These three activities are available for student choice throughout the week as regular instruction takes place.

- 1–2 days—The teacher chooses an activity from the menu to use with the entire class.

Suggested Forms

- All-purpose rubric
- Student-taught lesson rubric
- Free-choice proposal form

Name:_____ Date:_____

Mitosis and Meiosis

Directions: Check the boxes you plan to complete. They should form a tic-tac-toe across or down. All products are due by: _____.

☐ *Mitosis* Students have trouble remembering the order of the stages of mitosis and what occurs during each stage. Design a class lesson that teaches the stages of mitosis and their importance to the cell.	☐ *Meiosis* Meiosis is a multiple stage cell division process. Develop a board game that takes players on a journey through the various stages of meiosis. The questions should focus on the process and its importance.	☐ *Comparing Mitosis and Meiosis* Some teachers explain that meiosis is actually mitosis happening twice. Is this a correct assumption? Create a poster that shows why a teacher may say that and whether or not it is a true statement.
☐ *Comparing Mitosis and Meiosis* Draw a comic strip that shows the similarities and differences between mitosis and meiosis in a humorous way.	☐ **Free Choice on Mitosis** (Fill out your proposal form before beginning the free choice!)	☐ *Meiosis* Orchestrate a class model that allows students to demonstrate the stages of meiosis. Be sure to use important vocabulary terms like *haploid* and *diploid* when sharing your model.
☐ *Meiosis* Do all cells go through meiosis? Design an informational brochure for the process of meiosis that emphasizes its various stages, which cells experience the process, and its importance to all living things.	☐ *Comparing Mitosis and Meiosis* Write and perform a play in which a chromosome has to choose whether it wants to go through the processes of mitosis and meiosis.	☐ *Mitosis* You have been given the task to interview a centriole about its job and its importance to mitosis. Write your interview questions and provide creative yet reasonable responses to the questions.

Heredity: Punnett Square Practice

Three-Topic List Menu

Objectives Covered Through This Menu and These Activities

- Students will analyze and interpret visual representations of biological processes.
- Students will recognize how traits, genes, and alleles are related.
- Students will explain the relationship between genes and chromosomes.
- Students will predict the phenotype of an organism given its genotype.
- Students will indicate whether a genotype is homozygous or heterozygous.
- Students will use Punnett squares to solve genetic problems.
- Students will practice crosses with codominance, incomplete dominance, and ex-linked traits.

Materials Needed by Students for Completion

- Poster board or large white paper
- Microsoft PowerPoint or other slideshow software

Special Notes on the Use of This Menu

- This menu is a little different than the others in this book as it incorporates varying levels of Punnett square practice with the creation of products. There is an answer key provided for all of the specific crosses. All of the dominance information (as well as additional information for students who are creating their own crosses) is listed on the menu.

Time Frame

- 1–2 weeks—Students are given the menu as the unit is started, and the guidelines and point expectations are discussed. Students will need to earn 100 points for 100%, although there is an opportunity for extra credit if the teacher would like to use another target number. Because this menu covers three topics in depth, the teacher may choose to only go over the options for the topic being covered first; the students place check marks in the boxes next to the activities they are most interested in completing. As instruction continues, additional explanation of the new topic activities can be provided. Once students have access to the entire menu, teachers will need to set aside a few moments to sign the agreement at the bottom of the page with each student. As students complete activities, they will be submitted to the teacher for grading.

- 1–2 days—The teacher chooses an activity or product from an objective to use with the entire class during that lesson time.

Suggested Forms

- All-purpose rubric
- Proposal form for point-based products

Heredity: Punnett Square Practice

Guidelines:

1. You may complete as many of the problems listed as you can within the time period.
2. You may choose any combination of problems, but you **must** complete at least one problem from each topic area.
3. Your goal is _____ points. You may earn up to _____ points extra credit.
4. You must share your plan with your teacher by _____.
5. Problems may be completed at any time during the working time period. They will be graded and recorded on this sheet as you continue to work, so keep it safe!

Dominance Chart

The following chart shares the dominant traits for different living things.

Humans	Mice	Pea Plants
Brown eyes	Black eyes	Smooth peas (wrinkled)
Free ear lobes	Black fur	Pink flowers (white)
Can roll tongue		Unripe green pods (yellow)
Dimples	**Guinea Pigs**	Axil flowers (terminal)
Freckles	Rough coat	Tall stems (drawf)
Hairy ears	Long hair	Inflated pea pod shape (constricted)

Topic	Plan to Do	Activity to Complete	Point Value	Date Completed	Points Earned
Basic		Create a windowpane for the important terms used in genetic crosses.	10		
		Make a poster that shows how an offspring inherits alleles from each of its parents. Use mice in your example.	10		
		Use a Punnett square to create your own single trait cross for a pea plant. Write a word sentence explaining your cross and include its genotypic and phenotypic rations.	15		
		Cross 1: A heterozygous smooth pea plant is crossed with a homozygous wrinkled pea plant. Use a Punnett square to show the genotypic and phenotypic ratios for this cross.	15		
		Cross 2: A homozygous person who cannot roll his tongue is crossed with a purebred person who can. Use a Punnett square to show the genotypic and phenotypic ratios for this cross.	15		
Intermediate (Part 1)		Make a Venn diagram to compare and contrast incomplete dominance and codominance.	20		
		Cross 3: A white flowered pea plant that is heterozygous tall is crossed with a dwarf, heterozygous pink pea plant. Using a Punnett square, show the phenotypic and genotypic ratios for this cross. If 120 seeds are produced, how many of the seeds should produce dwarf pink plants?	20		
		Cross 4: A hybrid long-hair female guinea pig with a smooth coat is crossed with a short-hair, smooth-coated male guinea pig. Using a Punnett square, show the phenotypic and genotypic ratios for this cross. If a guinea pig has six babies, how many babies should resemble the mother?	20		

Name:_____ Date:_____

Heredity: Punnett Square Practice, *continued*

Dominance Chart

The following chart shares the dominant traits for different living things.

Incomplete Dominance

Humans: Straight hair

Flowers: Red

Guinea pigs: Dark hair

Rabbits: Short fur

Codominance

AB blood types

Coat color in cats
(black, tan, tabby)

For Pea Plants

Smooth peas (wrinkled)

Pink flowers (white)

Unripe green pods (yellow)

Axil flowers (terminal)

Tall stems (drawf)

Inflated pea pod (constricted)

Sex-Linked traits

X^B—not color blind

X^H—no hemophilia

X^R—red eyes in fruit flies

X^D—hearing in cats

Topic	Plan to Do	Activity to Complete	Point Value	Date Completed	Points Earned
Intermediate (Part 2)		Design a cross using incomplete dominance. Create three facts and a fib about the cross you created.	25		
		Cross 5: A couple has three children; one has wavy hair and two have straight hair. What are the possible genotypes for the parents? Use a Punnett square to prove your hypothesis.	25		
		Cross 6: A person with Type O blood has a child with someone who is Type A. Is it possible for the child to be a universal donor? If so, what is the chance of this happening? Prove your hypothesis using a Punnett square.	25		
Advanced		Create a PowerPoint presentation that shows how hemophilia was passed throughout the royal family in England. Include a pedigree for at least three generations in your presentation.	30		
		Develop a three-generation pedigree for a sex-linked trait of your choice. Use Punnett squares to prove the offspring in each generation was possible.	30		
Any		**Free choice**—Submit a proposal form to your teacher for a product of your choice.			
		Total number of points you are planning to earn.		**Total points earned:**	

I am planning to complete _____ activities that could earn up to a total of _____ points.

Teacher's initials _____ Student's signature _____

Answer Key for Heredity: Punnett Square Practice Menu

Cross 1: A heterozygous smooth pea plant is crossed with a homozygous wrinkled pea plant. Use a Punnett square to show the genotypic and phenotypic ratios for this cross.

Genotypic Ratio: 1:1
Phenotypic Ratio: 1:1

	S	s
s	Ss	ss
s	Ss	ss

Cross 2: A homozygous person who cannot roll his tongue is crossed with a purebred person who can. Use a Punnett square to show the genotypic and phenotypic ratios for this cross.

Genotypic Ratio: 1:0
Phenotypic Ratio: 1:0

	r	r
R	Rr	Rr
R	Rr	Rr

Cross 3: A white flowered pea plant that is heterozygous tall is crossed with a dwarf, heterozygous pink pea plant. Using a Punnett square, show the phenotypic and genotypic ratios for this cross. If 120 seeds are produced, how many of the seeds should produce dwarf pink plants?

Genotypic Ratio: 1:1:1:1
Phenotypic Ratio: 1:1:1:1
Thirty seeds should be
    dwarf pink plants.

	pT	pT	pt	pt
Pt	PpTt	PpTt	Pptt	Pptt
pt	ppTt	ppTt	pptt	pptt
Pt	PpTt	PpTt	Pptt	Pptt
pt	ppTt	ppTt	pptt	pptt

Cross 4: A hybrid long-hair female guinea pig with a smooth coat is crossed with a short-hair, smooth-coated male guinea pig. Using a Punnett square, show the phenotypic and genotypic ratios for this cross. If a guinea pig has six babies, how many babies should resemble the mother?

Genotypic Ratio: 1:1
Phenotypic Ratio: 1:1
Three should resemble
    their mother.

	rL	rL	rl	rl
rl	rrLl	rrLl	rrll	rrll
rl	rrLl	rrLl	rrll	rrll
rl	rrLl	rrLl	rrll	rrll
rl	rrLl	rrLl	rrll	rrll

Cross 5: A couple has three children; one has wavy hair and two have straight hair. What are the possible genotypes for the parents? Use a Punnett square to prove your hypothesis.

One of the parents has to be heterozygous for straight hair; the other could be either homozygous or heterozygous for straight hair.

	S	s
S	SS	Ss
s	Ss	ss

	S	s
S	SS	Ss
S	SS	Ss

Cross 6: A person with Type O blood has a child with someone who is Type A. Is it possible for the child to be a universal donor? If so, what is the chance of this happening? Prove your hypothesis using a Punnett square.

It is only possible if the Type A parent is heterozygous. In which case, there is a 50% chance the child will be a universal donor.

	i	i
i^A	i^Ai	i^Ai
i^A	i^Ai	i^Ai

	i	i
i^A	i^Ai	i^Ai
i	ii	ii

Mutations

20-50-80 Menu

Objectives Covered Through This Menu and These Activities

- Students will explain different types of mutations, how they occur, and their possible impact on organisms.
- Students will explain how DNA's structure allows it to code for genes and replicate.
- Students will describe how a mutation is a change in the DNA or chromosome of an organism and the possible effects on an organism or population.

Materials Needed by Students for Completion

- Poster board or large white paper
- Blank index cards (for trading cards)
- Graph paper or Internet access (for crossword puzzles)
- Recycled materials (for models)
- Materials for board games (folders, colored cards, etc.)
- Microsoft PowerPoint or other slideshow software
- DVD or VHS recorder (for public service announcements)

Special Notes on the Use of This Menu

- This menu gives students the opportunity to create a public service announcement. Although students enjoy producing their own videos, there often are difficulties obtaining the equipment and scheduling the use of a video recorder. These activities can be modified by allowing students to act out the public service announcement (like a play) or, if students have the technology, allowing them to produce a webcam version of their product.
- This menu asks students to use recycled materials to create their models. This does not mean only plastic and paper; instead, students should focus on using materials in new ways. It works well if a box is started for recycled contributions at the beginning of the school year. That way, students always have access to these types of materials.

Time Frame

- 1–2 weeks—Students are given a menu as the unit is started, and the teacher discusses all of the product options on the menu. As the different options are discussed, students will choose the activities they are most interested in completing so they meet their goal of 100 points. As the lessons progress, the teacher and students refer back to the menu options associated with the content being taught.

- 1–2 days—The teacher chooses an activity or product from the menu to use with the entire class.

Suggested Forms

- All-purpose rubric
- Proposal form for point-based projects

Name:_____   Date:_____

Mutations

Directions: Choose at least two activities from the menu below. The activities must total 100 points. Place a check mark next to each box to show which activities you will complete. All activities must be completed by _____.

20 Points

- ❐ Prepare a windowpane that shows the different types of mutations that can result. Include a brief explanation for how each takes place.
- ❐ Write a crossword puzzle that focuses on different types of mutations and the consequences when this mutation happens.

50 Points

- ❐ Create a set of trading cards for diseases or disorders caused by mutations. In addition to describing the disease, be sure to include how the mutation takes place.
- ❐ Using recycled materials, make a model that can be used to demonstrate at least three different ways that mutations can take place. Use your model to demonstrate the mutations.
- ❐ Design a mutation board game in which players start with specific DNA strands and run the risk of mutating as they go through the steps that lead to protein synthesis as they play the game. Be creative with your mutation possibilities.
- ❐ **Free choice**—Submit a proposal form to your teacher for a product of your choice.

80 Points

- ❐ Choose a disease or disorder caused by a genetic mutation that, although it affects many people, has no outward signs. Research this disease, its cause, and its symptoms. Create a stand-alone PowerPoint presentation to share your information with others.
- ❐ Select a disease or disorder caused by a genetic mutation that changes the physical appearance of the person who suffers from it. Record a public service announcement educating your classmates about the disease, its symptoms, and what causes the mutation. Your video should help others understand why someone with this disease may look different.

© *Prufrock Press Inc. • Differentiating Instruction With Menus: Biology • Grades 9–12*

CHAPTER 8

Ecology

Charles Darwin and His Voyage

Tic-Tac-Toe Menu

Objectives Covered Through This Menu and These Activities

- Students share the events that led up Darwin's voyage.
- Students will investigate the religious, philosophical, and historical impact of his voyage and findings.
- Students will understand what life was like in the 1800s.
- Students will recognize that natural selection is the primary process for evolutionary change.
- Students will recognize the factors that lead to speciation.
- Students will demonstrate an understanding that evolutionary theory provides an explanation for the diversity of life on Earth.

Materials Needed by Students for Completion

- Poster board or large white paper
- Internet access (for WebQuests)
- Microsoft PowerPoint or other slideshow software
- Materials for three-dimensional timelines
- Materials for bulletin board displays

Special Notes on the Use of This Menu

- This menu allows students to create a bulletin board display. Some classrooms may only have one bulletin board, so the teacher can divide the board into sections, or additional classroom wall or hall space can be sectioned off for the creation of these displays. Students can plan their display based on the amount of space they are assigned.
- This menu allows students to create a WebQuest. There are multiple versions and templates for WebQuests available on the Internet. Teachers should decide whether to specify a certain format or allow students to create one of their own choosing.

Time Frame

- 2–3 weeks—Students are given the menu as the unit is started. As the teacher presents lessons throughout the week, he or she should refer back to the menu options associated with that content. The teacher will go over all of the options for that content and have students place check marks in the boxes that represent the activities they are most interested in completing. As students choose activities, they should complete a column or a row. When students complete this pattern, they have completed one activity from each content area, learning style, or level of Bloom's revised taxonomy, depending on the design of the menu.

- 1 week—At the start of the unit, the teacher chooses the three activities he or she feels are most valuable for students. Stations can be set up in the classroom. These three activities are available for student choice throughout the week as regular instruction takes place.
- 1–2 days—The teacher chooses an activity from the menu to use with the entire class.

Suggested Forms

- All-purpose rubric
- Free-choice proposal form

Charles Darwin and His Voyage

Directions: Check the boxes you plan to complete. They should form a tic-tac-toe across or down. All products are due by: _____.

☐ *The Voyage* Create a three-dimensional timeline that begins when Darwin asked for support for his 5-year voyage until *Origin of Species* was published.	☐ *Life in Darwin's Time* Design a WebQuest that has questors discovering the political, scientific, and cultural events of Darwin's time. Be sure to include information about world events that were occurring as well.	☐ *Religious Impacts of His Findings* Consider the impact Darwin's findings had on religious views during his time period. Create an advertisement that shares how the church viewed his discoveries.
☐ *Philosophical Impacts of His Findings* Darwin's idea of the randomness of natural selection has created a philosophical impact that is still felt today. Research this impact and write an essay that shares your findings.	☐ **Free Choice on Charles Darwin's Voyage** (Fill out your proposal form before beginning the free choice!)	☐ *Life in Darwin's Time* Consider all of the different aspects of Darwin's time period. Design a bulletin board display that shares the political, scientific, and cultural climate during the time when Darwin first asked for support for his voyage. Did the climate change after his return? Be sure to include any changes in your display as well.
☐ *Life in Darwin's Time* How has life changed since Darwin's lifetime? Make a Venn diagram that compares and contrasts life in Darwin's time with a biologist's life today. Go deeper than obvious technological differences.	☐ *Historical Impacts of His Findings* Darwin's research and discoveries caused many debates. The outcomes of these debates shaped history in many ways. Select a topic that was debated and perform a play of the debate with a classmate.	☐ *The Voyage* Using PowerPoint, design a diary that shares information about Darwin's 5-year voyage on the H.M.S. *Beagle*. Include photos, drawings, and maps as well as realistic diary entries to document his journey.

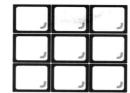

Biodiversity

Game Show Menu

Objectives Covered Through This Menu and These Activities

- Students will identify examples of biodiversity at the genetic, species, and/or ecosystem levels.
- Students will identify how humans benefit from biodiversity.
- Students will understand human impacts on biodiversity, including invasive species, population growth, and pollution.
- Students will recognize evolution as change over time.
- Students will recognize that natural selection is the primary process for evolutionary change.
- Students will recognize the factors that lead to speciation.
- Students will demonstrate an understanding that evolutionary theory provides an explanation for the diversity of life on Earth.

Materials Needed by Students for Completion

- Poster board or large white paper
- Blank index cards (for mobiles)
- Coat hangers (for mobiles)
- String (for mobiles)
- Recycled materials (for models and dioramas)
- Ruler (for comic strips)
- Scrapbooking materials
- Microsoft PowerPoint or other slideshow software
- DVD or VHS recorder (for videos)
- Internet access (for WebQuests)

Special Notes on the Use of This Menu

- This menu gives students the opportunity to create a video. Although students enjoy producing their own videos, there often are difficulties obtaining the equipment and scheduling the use of a video recorder. This activity can be modified by allowing students to act out the video (like a play) or, if students have the technology, allowing them to produce a webcam version of their product.
- This menu asks students to use recycled materials to create their dioramas and models. This does not mean only plastic and paper; instead, students should focus on using materials in new ways. It

works well if a box is started for recycled contributions at the beginning of the school year. That way, students always have access to these types of materials.

- This menu allows students to create a WebQuest. There are multiple versions and templates for WebQuests available on the Internet. Teachers should decide whether to specify a certain format or allow students to create one of their own choosing.

Time Frame

- 2–3 weeks—Students are given their menu as the unit is started and the guidelines and point expectations are discussed. As lessons are taught throughout the unit, students and the teacher can refer back to the options associated with that topic. The teacher will go over all of the options for the topic being covered and will have students place check marks in the boxes next to the activities they are most interested in completing. As teaching continues throughout the 2–3 weeks, activities are discussed, chosen, and submitted for grading.
- 1 week—At the beginning of the unit, the teacher chooses an activity from each area he or she feels would be most valuable for students. Stations can be set up in the classroom. These activities are available for student choice throughout the week as regular instruction takes place.
- 1–2 days—The teacher chooses an activity from an objective to use with the entire class during lesson time.

Suggested Forms

- All-purpose rubric
- Proposal form for point-based products

Guidelines for Biodiversity Game Show Menu

- You must choose at least one activity from each topic area.
- You may not do more than two activities in any one topic area for credit. (You are, of course, welcome to do more than two for your own investigation.)
- Grading will be ongoing, so turn in products as you complete them.
- All free-choice proposals must be turned in and approved *prior* to working on a free-choice product.
- You must earn 120 points for a 100%. You may earn extra credit up to _____ points.
- You must show your teacher your plan for completion by: _____.

Name:_____ Date:_____

Biodiversity

What Is Biodiversity?	Evolution	Distribution	Extinction	Human Impact	Points for Each Level
☐ Create a poster to show biodiversity. Your poster may have as many pictures or drawings as you like but cannot have more than five words. (15 pts.)	☐ Make a mind map to show different ways that organisms can evolve. (10 pts.)	☐ Write an acrostic for the word *distribution*. Use each letter to share an action that impacts the distribution of species. (15 pts.)	☐ Assemble a mobile that shares the different types of extinctions with at least three examples of each. (10 pts.)	☐ Consider the different impacts that humans have on biodiversity. Using recycled materials, build a diorama that shows two of these impacts. (10 pts.)	15 points
☐ Design a map to show the biodiversity in your state. Write five questions about what it shows to accompany your map. (25 pts.)	☐ Use recycled materials to build a model that could be used to demonstration speciation. Use your model to demonstrate speciation for at least two species. (20 pts.)	☐ Research the term *distribution hot spots*. Prepare a PowerPoint presentation to share two different hot spots of species and share the reasons scientists believe they exist. (20 pts.)	☐ Investigate the mass extinctions that are believed to have happened on Earth. Create an extinction scrapbook detailing each event and its impact on the biodiversity at the time. (25 pts.)	☐ Draw a comic strip that shares the response of a local organism to a human activity that is starting to have an impact on its life. (20 pts.)	25 points
☐ Do you think there is a lot of biodiversity where you live? Create a video in which you visit various local locations, make observations, and share your conclusions about the biodiversity levels. (30 pts.)	☐ What species of living things have the greatest diversity because of evolution? Prepare a WebQuest to take questors through different species (don't forget plants!) that demonstrate significant diversity. (30 pts.)	☐ Create class game that will teach your classmates about the forces that impact distribution of organisms. (30 pts.)	☐ Select a mass extinction other than the end of the Mesozoic Era. Write a children's book about the event and its impact on the biosphere. Include information on those who survived as well as those who suffered extinction. (30 pts.)	☐ Research the impacts humans are having on a local organism and perform a debate in play form between the organism and the humans making the impact. (30 pts.)	30 points
Free Choice (prior approval) (25–50 pts.)	Free Choice (prior approval) (25–50 pts.)	Free Choice (prior approval) (25–50 pts.)	Free Choice (prior approval) (25–50 pts.)	Free Choice (prior approval) (25–50 pts.)	25–50 points
Total:	Total:	Total:	Total:	Total:	Total Grade:

Ecology

Three-Topic List Menu

Objectives Covered Through This Menu and These Activities

- Students will distinguish between different levels of organization within the biosphere.
- Students will apply concepts of the interdependence of living and nonliving components of the environment.
- Students will predict the effects on an ecosystem given limitations and disruptions.
- Students will recognize the relationship between organisms and the flow of energy in an ecosystem.
- Students will apply concepts of interactions among organisms within an ecosystem.

Materials Needed by Students for Completion

- Poster board or large white paper
- Blank index cards (for trading cards)
- Materials for board games (folders, colored cards, etc.)
- Materials for bulletin board displays
- DVD or VHS recorder (for news reports)
- Recycled materials (for models)
- Microsoft PowerPoint or other slideshow software

Special Notes on the Use of This Menu

- This menu gives students the opportunity to create a news report. Although students enjoy producing their own videos, there often are difficulties obtaining the equipment and scheduling the use of a video recorder. This activity can be modified by allowing students to act out the news report (like a play) or, if students have the technology, allowing them to produce a webcam version of their product.
- This menu asks students to use recycled materials to create their models. This does not mean only plastic and paper; instead, students should focus on using materials in new ways. It works well if a box is started for recycled contributions at the beginning of the school year. That way, students always have access to these types of materials.
- This menu allows students to create a bulletin board display. Some classrooms may only have one bulletin board, so the teacher can

divide the board into sections, or additional classroom wall or hall space can be sectioned off for the creation of these displays. Students can plan their display based on the amount of space they are assigned.

Time Frame

- 1–2 weeks—Students are given the menu as the unit is started, and the guidelines and point expectations are discussed. Students will need to earn 100 points for 100%, although there is an opportunity for extra credit if the teacher would like to use another target number. Because this menu covers three topics in depth, the teacher may choose to only go over the options for the topic being covered first; the students place check marks in the boxes next to the activities they are most interested in completing. As instruction continues, additional explanation of the new topic activities can be provided. Once students have access to the entire menu, teachers will need to set aside a few moments to sign the agreement at the bottom of the page with each student. As students complete activities, they will be submitted to the teacher for grading.
- 1–2 days—The teacher chooses an activity or product from an objective to use with the entire class during that lesson time.

Suggested Forms

- All-purpose rubric
- Proposal form for point-based products

Name:_____ Date:_____

Ecology

Guidelines:

1. You may complete as many of the activities listed as you can within the time period.
2. You may choose any combination of activities, but you **must** complete at least one activity from each topic area.
3. Your goal is 100 points. You may earn up to _____ points extra credit.
4. You may be as creative as you like within the guidelines listed below.
5. You must share your plan with your teacher by _____.
6. Activities may be turned in at any time during the working time period. They will be graded and recorded on this sheet as you continue to work, so keep it safe!

Topic	Plan to Do	Activity to Complete	Point Value	Date Completed	Points Earned
Interdependence		Create a set of trading cards for a specific ecosystem that includes examples of the plants, animals, and abiotic factors of that ecosystem.	15		
		Design a folded quiz book that asks questions about the interdependence and symbiotic relationships found in a specific ecosystem.	15		
		Make an ecosystem board game in which players move through your ecosystem encountering both biotic and abiotic factors and examples of interdependence within the ecosystem.	20		
		Biotic and abiotic factors impact an ecosystem. Which factor has the greatest impact on your ecosystem? Create a brochure about this factor and how the ecosystem would be impacted if that factor ceased to exist.	20		
Limiting Factors		Make a windowpane that shares various types of disruptions that might impact an ecosystem.	10		
		Design a questionnaire to determine what people know about the most significant limiting factor in your area. Gather and share the results.	20		
		Create a class game to demonstrate how limiting factors can affect a population.	25		
		When a nonnative consumer or predator is introduced into an ecosystem, there can be both beneficial and disastrous effects. Research how nonnative species have had an impact on an ecosystem. Write and perform a news report that shares your discovery as well as whether or not you support this practice.	25		
Energy Flow		Using recycled materials, build a model that uses manipulatives to show how energy is transferred from the sun through an ecosystem.	15		
		Make a poster that shows how energy moves through an ecosystem of your choice. Do not use local examples.	15		
		Is there a limit to the number of trophic levels an ecosystem can support? Design a PowerPoint presentation that answers this question using real-world examples.	20		
		Research gross primary productivity (GPP) and net primary productivity (NPP). Create a bulletin board display that shares different things that impact them and the importance of knowing this information.	25		
Any		**Free choice**—Submit a proposal form to your teacher for a product of your choice.			
		Total number of points you are planning to earn.		**Total points earned:**	

I am planning to complete _____ activities that could earn up to a total of _____ points.

Teacher's initials _____ Student's signature _____

CHAPTER 9

In-Depth Studies

In-Depth Study: A Biome

Challenge List Menu

Objectives Covered Through This Menu and These Activities
- Students will apply concepts of the interdependence of living and non-living components of the environment.
- Students will predict the effects on an ecosystem given limitations and disruptions.
- Students will recognize the relationship between organisms and the flow of energy in an ecosystem.
- Students will apply concepts of interactions among organisms within an ecosystem.

Materials Needed by Students for Completion
- Poster board or large white paper
- Large blank or lined index cards (for recipe cards)
- Blank index cards (for trading cards)
- Magazines (for collages)
- Internet access (for WebQuests)
- DVD or VHS recorder (for videos and news reports)
- Microsoft PowerPoint or other slideshow software

Special Notes on the Use of This Menu
- This menu is meant to be a generic menu that can be used to study any biome in depth. This menu can be used to accommodate various curricular options; teachers can have all students study the same biome or assign different biomes to different students.
- This menu gives students the opportunity to create a video and a news report. Although students enjoy producing their own videos, there often are difficulties obtaining the equipment and scheduling the use of a video recorder. This activity can be modified by allowing students to act out the video or news report (like a play) or, if students have the technology, allowing them to produce a webcam version of their product.
- This menu allows students to create a WebQuest. There are multiple versions and templates for WebQuests available on the Internet. Teachers should decide whether to specify a certain format or allow students to create one of their own choosing.

Time Frame

- 1–2 weeks—Students are given the menu as the unit is started, and the guidelines and point expectations are discussed. Students will need to earn 100 points for 100%, although there is an opportunity for extra credit if the teacher would like to use another target number. Because this menu covers one topic in depth, the teacher will go over all of the options for the topic being covered and have students place check marks in the boxes next to the activities they are most interested in completing. Teachers will need to set aside a few moments to sign the agreement at the bottom of the page with each student. As students complete activities, they will be submitted to the teacher for grading.
- 1–2 days—The teacher chooses an activity or product from an objective to use with the entire class during that lesson time.

Suggested Forms

- All-purpose rubric
- Proposal form for point-based products

Name:_____   Date:_____

In-Depth Study: A Biome

Guidelines:

1. You may complete as many of the activities listed as you can within the time period.
2. You may choose any combination of activities.
3. Your goal is 100 points. You may earn up to _____ points extra credit.
4. You may be as creative as you like within the guidelines listed below.
5. You must share your plan with your teacher by _____.
6. Activities may be turned in at any time during the working time period. They will be graded and recorded on this sheet as you continue to work, so keep it safe!

Plan to Do	Activity to Complete	Point Value	Date Completed	Points Earned
	Make a windowpane for the words *biotic* and *abiotic* as well as the different types of symbiotic relationships. Include an example from your biome for each relationship.	10		
	Find at least two sources of information about your biome. Use these sources to create a poster Wordle about your biome.	15		
	Consider all aspects of your biome and design a recipe card for creating your biome.	15		
	Assemble a collage of pictures and words that represent your biome. Use these pictures and words to write an essay describing your biome in detail.	15		
	Create a set of trading cards for your ecosystem that includes examples of the biotic and abiotic things found in your biome.	15		
	Complete a Venn diagram to compare and contrast your biome with another biome.	20		
	Draw a mural that could represent your biome. Be sure to include aspects that are specific to just your biome.	20		
	Design a folded quiz book that asks questions about the interdependence and symbiotic relationships found in your biome.	20		
	Perform a song or rap about the unique qualities of your biome.	20		
	Create a brochure about the most biotic or abiotic factor in your biome and how the ecosystem would be impacted if that factor ceased to exist.	25		
	Design a WebQuest for your biome. Include at least one video with footage of an important aspect of your biome.	25		
	A large ecological disruption has just occurred in your biome. Write and perform a news report to share what has happened and how it will impact the biome in the upcoming year(s).	30		
	Create a video that shares a 24-hour period in your biome.	30		
	Identify one native pest species in your biome and one nonnative species that could be introduced to address this pest. Design a PowerPoint presentation that supports or refutes the idea of the introduction of this species in your biome. Be sure to include the benefits and drawbacks!	30		
	Free choice—Submit a proposal form to your teacher for a product of your choice.			
	Total number of points you are planning to earn.	**Total points earned:**		

I am planning to complete _____ activities that could earn up to a total of _____ points.

Teacher's initials _____   Student's signature _____

© Prufrock Press Inc. • *Differentiating Instruction With Menus: Biology • Grades 9–12*

In-Depth Study:
A Division of Taxonomy

20-50-80 Menu

Objectives Covered Through This Menu and These Activities

- Students will identify traits that classify organisms into different taxonomies.
- Students will understand how taxonomies are developed.

Materials Needed by Students for Completion

- Poster board or large white paper
- Blank index cards (for mobiles and trading cards)
- Coat hangers (for mobiles)
- String (for mobiles)
- Materials for three-dimensional timelines
- Scrapbooking materials
- Internet access (for WebQuests)

Special Notes on the Use of This Menu

- This menu is meant to be a generic menu that can be used to study any taxonomy level in depth. This menu can be used to accommodate various curricular options; teachers can have all students study the same level or assign different levels to different students.
- This menu allows students to create a WebQuest. There are multiple versions and templates for WebQuests available on the Internet. Teachers should decide whether to specify a certain format or allow students to create one of their own choosing.

Time Frame

- 1–2 weeks—Students are given a menu as the unit is started, and the teacher discusses all of the product options on the menu. As the different options are discussed, students will choose the activities they are most interested in completing so they meet their goal of 100 points. As the lessons progress, the teacher and students refer back to the menu options associated with the content being taught.
- 1–2 days—The teacher chooses an activity or product from the menu to use with the entire class.

Suggested Forms
- All-purpose rubric
- Proposal form for point-based projects

In-Depth Study: A Division of Taxonomy

Directions: Choose at least two activities from the menu below. The activities must total 100 points. Place a check mark next to each box to show which activities you will complete. All activities must be completed by _____.

---

20 Points

❑ Create an acrostic for the name of your taxonomy division. Write traits, properties, or organisms that can be found in your rank for each letter.

❑ Research the specific way your division is written in an organism's name. Assemble a mobile that shows recognizable organisms from your division with their scientific names.

---

50 Points

❑ Develop a set of trading cards for each of the divisions you contain. For example, if your division is Kingdom Animalia, you would create trading cards for the different phyla within it.

❑ Brainstorm an advertisement for your division that shares the unique qualities that separates it from other divisions of the same rank.

❑ Design a taxonomy scrapbook filled with organisms contained in your division. Under each organism, include its properties that categorize it within your division.

❑ **Free choice**—Submit a proposal form to your teacher for a product of your choice.

---

80 Points

❑ Design a WebQuest about your division of taxonomy. It should teach others about the unique qualities of the organisms within it and include photos and features of these organisms. You should also explain how the organisms are divided further within your division (e.g., if you have the Phyla Chordata, you would include the classes within it).

❑ Sometimes the divisions within the currently accepted taxonomy are debated and changed based on new research. Research your division to discover how it has evolved (it may even now be under debate). Build a three-dimensional timeline that shares all of the events that have taken place in the shaping of your division since Aristotle's first division of organisms.

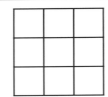

In-Depth Study: An Organ

Tic-Tac-Toe Menu

Objectives Covered Through This Menu and These Activities
- Students will analyze and interpret visual representations of biological processes.
- Students will identify the structures and their functions for an organ in an organism.
- Students will be able to state how the organ being studied is interdependent with other organs in the organism.

Materials Needed by Students for Completion
- Poster board or large white paper
- Internet access (for WebQuests)
- Aluminum foil (for quiz boards)
- Holiday lights (for quiz boards)
- Wires (for quiz boards)
- Microsoft PowerPoint or other slideshow software
- Organ Structure Cube template
- DVD or VHS recorder (for infomercials)
- Graph paper or Internet access (for crossword puzzles)
- Recycled materials (for models)

Special Notes on the Use of This Menu
- This menu is meant to be a generic menu that can be used to study any organ in depth. This menu can be used to accommodate various curricular options; teachers can have all students study the same organ or assign different organs to different students.
- This menu gives students the opportunity to create an infomercial. Although students enjoy producing their own videos, there often are difficulties obtaining the equipment and scheduling the use of a video recorder. This activity can be modified by allowing students to act out the infomercial (like a play) or, if students have the technology, allowing them to produce a webcam version of their product.
- This menu asks students to use recycled materials to create their model of an organ. This does not mean only plastic and paper; instead, students should focus on using materials in new ways. It works well if a box is started for recycled contributions at the beginning of the

school year. That way, students always have access to these types of materials.

- This menu gives students an opportunity to create a quiz board. A student-friendly information sheet that offers the steps for constructing a quiz board is available at http://www.cesiscience.org/attachments/article/100/QuizBoardDirections.pdf.
- This menu allows students to create a WebQuest. There are multiple versions and templates for WebQuests available on the Internet. Teachers should decide whether to specify a certain format or allow students to create one of their own choosing.

Time Frame

- 2–3 weeks—Students are given the menu as the unit is started. As the teacher presents lessons throughout the week, he or she should refer back to the menu options associated with that content. The teacher will go over all of the options for that content and have students place check marks in the boxes that represent the activities they are most interested in completing. As students choose activities, they should complete a column or a row. When students complete this pattern, they have completed one activity from each content area, learning style, or level of Bloom's revised taxonomy, depending on the design of the menu.
- 1 week–At the start of the unit, the teacher chooses the three activities he or she feels are most valuable for students. Stations can be set up in the classroom. These three activities are available for student choice throughout the week as regular instruction takes place.
- 1–2 days—The teacher chooses an activity from the menu to use with the entire class.

Suggested Forms

- All-purpose rubric
- Free-choice proposal form

Name:_____ Date:_____

In-Depth Study: An Organ

Directions: Check the boxes you plan to complete. They should form a tic-tac-toe across or down. All products are due by: _____.

☐ *Function*	☐ *Structure*	☐ *Interdependence*
Design a WebQuest that focuses on the functions this organ performs for the organism. Include at least one website with videos or pictures that demonstrate how this function takes place.	Build a quiz board that has users matching the names of this organ's structures with the structures themselves.	This organ has been nominated for the Most Important Contribution Award, or MICA. Design a PowerPoint presentation for this award that shows all of the impacts the organ has on other organs or organ systems.
☐ *Interdependence*	☐ **Free Choice on the Organ's Function** (Fill out your proposal form before beginning the free choice!)	☐ *Structure*
Draw a mind map that has the organ in the middle. Then share all of the organs and organ systems that it impacts in your map. Include how each is impacted on your drawing.		Create a product cube to share the important structures of this organ. On each side, include how the structure is specific to this organ and how each helps it with its specialized function.
☐ *Structure*	☐ *Interdependence*	☐ *Function*
Create a crossword puzzle for the different structures found in this organ.	An organism's body can sometimes compensate when an organ stops working. Record an infomercial about how other organs or organ systems will be impacted if this organ stops working or does not work as efficiently as it should.	Use recycled materials to build a model that demonstrates the function of your organ. Your model does not have to look the organ; it needs to show the function it performs for the organism.

Organ Structure Cube

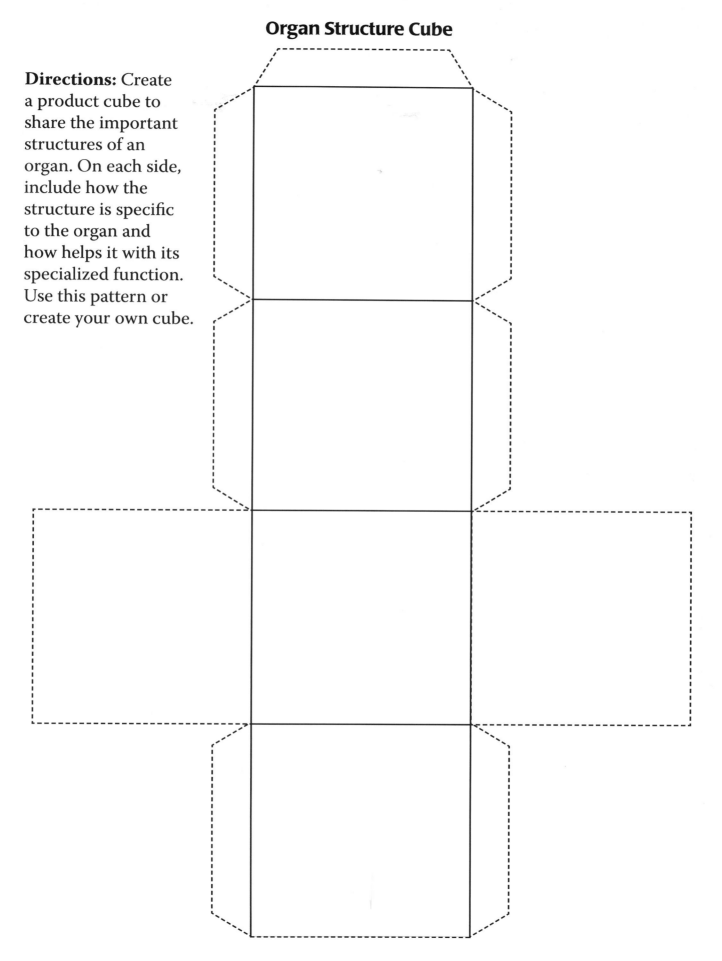

Directions: Create a product cube to share the important structures of an organ. On each side, include how the structure is specific to the organ and how helps it with its specialized function. Use this pattern or create your own cube.

In-Depth Study: An Organ System

Three-Topic List Menu

Objectives Covered Through This Menu and These Activities

- Students will analyze and interpret visual representations of biological processes.
- Students will identify the structures and their functions for an organ system in an organism.
- Students will be able to state how the organ system being studied is interdependent with other organ systems in the organism.

Materials Needed by Students for Completion

- Poster board or large white paper
- Blank index cards (for mobiles and trading cards)
- Coat hangers (for mobiles)
- String (for mobiles)
- Recycled materials (for models)
- Materials for board games (folders, colored cards, etc.)
- Microsoft PowerPoint or other slideshow software
- Scrapbooking materials
- DVD or VHS recorder (for commercials)
- Newspapers or access to online newspapers

Special Notes on the Use of This Menu

- This menu is meant to be a generic menu that can be used to study any organ system in depth. This menu can be used to accommodate various curricular options; teachers can have all students study the same organ system or assign different organ systems to different students.
- This menu asks students to use recycled materials to create their models. This does not mean only plastic and paper; instead, students should focus on using materials in new ways. It works well if a box is started for recycled contributions at the beginning of the school year. That way, students always have access to these types of materials.
- This menu allows students to create a bulletin board display. Some classrooms may only have one bulletin board, so the teacher can divide the board into sections, or additional classroom wall or hall space can be sectioned off for the creation of these displays. Students can plan their display based on the amount of space they are assigned.

Time Frame

- 1–2 weeks—Students are given the menu as the unit is started, and the guidelines and point expectations are discussed. Students will need to earn 100 points for 100%, although there is an opportunity for extra credit if the teacher would like to use another target number. Because this menu covers three topics in depth, the teacher may choose to only go over the options for the topic being covered first; the students place check marks in the boxes next to the activities they are most interested in completing. As instruction continues, additional explanation of the new topic activities can be provided. Once students have access to the entire menu, teachers will need to set aside a few moments to sign the agreement at the bottom of the page with each student. As students complete activities, they will be submitted to the teacher for grading.
- 1–2 days—The teacher chooses an activity or product from an objective to use with the entire class during that lesson time.

Suggested Forms

- All-purpose rubric
- Proposal form for point-based products

Name:_____ Date:_____

In-Depth Study: An Organ System

Guidelines:
1. You may complete as many of the activities listed as you can within the time period.
2. You may choose any combination of activities, but you **must** complete at least one activity from each topic area.
3. Your goal is 100 points. You may earn up to _____ points extra credit.
4. You may be as creative as you like within the guidelines listed below.
5. You must share your plan with your teacher by _____.
6. Activities may be turned in at any time during the working time period. They will be graded and recorded on this sheet as you continue to work, so keep it safe!

Topic	Plan to Do	Activity to Complete	Point Value	Date Completed	Points Earned
Structure		Assemble a mobile of the different organs found in this system with the functions of each.	10		
		Create a set of trading cards for the organs found within this organ system.	15		
		Using recycled materials, build a model of this organ system with its organs.	20		
		Design a commercial for what is viewed as the least important part of this organ system. Share why this organ is important to the success of the system.	25		
Function		Make a flipbook with the organs in this organ system on the top flap and the function of each inside. Include two sentences that state the function of the organ system as a whole.	10		
		Design a board game in which players travel through your organ system answering questions about its function.	20		
		Write a children's book to teach young children about the structures in your organ system and how they function together to serve the organism.	20		
		Find two articles about diseases or disorders that can affect this organ system. Create a PowerPoint presentation to share how each affects the organ system.	25		
Interdependence		Complete a Venn diagram to compare and contrast this organ system to another system in the organism.	15		
		Create an interdependence scrapbook with a page for each organ system in your organism. On each page, share how this organ system contributes to the success of the other organ system on that page.	20		
		Keep an hourly diary or journal for 5 hours in the life of this organ system. Include what all of the organs contribute as well as all of the other organ systems it works with during that time.	25		
Any		**Free choice**—Submit a proposal form to your teacher for a product of your choice.			
		Total number of points you are planning to earn.		**Total points earned:**	

I am planning to complete _____ activities that could earn up to a total of _____ points.

Teacher's initials _____ Student's signature _____

References

Anderson, L. W., & Krathwohl, D. R. (Eds.). (2001). *A taxonomy for learning, teaching, and assessing: A revision of Bloom's taxonomy of educational objectives.* New York, NY: Allyn & Bacon.

Keen, D. (2001). *Talent in the new millennium: Report on year one of the programme.* Retrieved from http://www.aare.edu.au/01pap/kee01007.htm

Magner, L. (2000). Reaching all children through differentiated assessment: The 2-5-8 plan. *Gifted Child Today, 23*(3), 48–50.

About the Author

After teaching science for more than 15 years, both overseas and in the U.S., **Laurie E. Westphal** now works as an independent gifted education and science consultant nationwide. She enjoys developing and presenting staff development on differentiation for various districts and conferences, working with teachers to assist them in planning and developing lessons to meet the needs of all students. Laurie currently resides in Houston, TX, and has made it her goal to convert as many teachers as she can to the differentiated lifestyle in the classroom and share her vision for real-world, product-based lessons that help all students become critical thinkers and effective problem solvers.

If you are interested in having Laurie speak at your next staff development day or conference, please visit her website, http://www.giftedconsultant.com, for additional information.

Next Generation Science Standards Alignment

This book aligns with an extensive number of the Next Generation Science Standards. Please visit https://www.prufrock.com/ccss.aspx to download a complete packet of the standards that align with each individual menu in this book.

Additional Titles by the Author

Laurie E. Westphal has written many books on using differentiation strategies in the classroom, providing teachers of grades K–12 with creative, engaging, ready-to-use resources. Among them are:

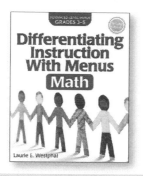 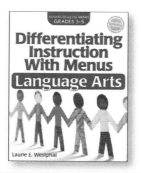  

Math, Language Arts, Science, and Social Studies volumes available for:

Differentiating Instruction With Menus, Grades K–2

Differentiating Instruction With Menus, Grades 3–5, Second Edition

Differentiating Instruction With Menus, Grades 6–8, Second Edition

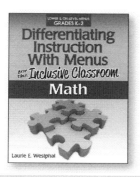 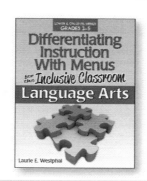  

Math, Language Arts, Science, and Social Studies volumes available for:

Differentiating Instruction With Menus for the Inclusive Classroom, Grades K–2

Differentiating Instruction With Menus for the Inclusive Classroom, Grades 3–5

Differentiating Instruction With Menus for the Inclusive Classroom, Grades 6–8

Literature for Every Learner, Grades 3–5; 6–8; and 9–12

Differentiating Instruction With Menus: Algebra I/II, Grades 9–12

Differentiating Instruction With Menus: Biology, Grades 9–12

For a current listing of Laurie's books, please visit Prufrock Press at http://www.prufrock.com.

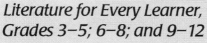